EDUCATING EXCEPTIONAL NEEDS YOUNGSTERS.

A RESOURCE FOR EDUCATORS, PARENTS, AND HEALTHCARE PRACTITIONERS: COUNSELING RAMIFICATIONS

First Published, 2023

AF368781

Noogul Digital Publishing

Contents

SECTION TWO:

GUIDANCE AND COUNSELING FOR LEARNERS WITH SPECIAL NEEDS

SECTION THREE:

INFORMATION COMMUNICATION TECHNOLOGY (ICT) FOR LEARNERS WITH SPECIAL NEEDS

SECTION FOUR:
REHABILITATION

DIAGNOSTIC AND REMEDIAL MATHEMATICS

DIAGNOSTIC AND REMEDIAL READING

SECTION TEN
DISORDERS OF LEARNING

SECTION ONE:

EARLY CHILDHOOD EDUCATION FOR CHILDREN WITH SPECIAL NEEDS.

The Philosophy of Pre-primary (Kindergarten) and Primary (Elementary) Education

Pre-primary (Basic/Elementary) is to prepare the children below school age for education in primary (Basic) schools. It should be noted that not all the scholars, have agreed on need for or, effectiveness of such early school education Programmes for subsequent educational development of children. Some early writers such as (Robinson, 1968) hold the view that young children are not mature enough to learn complex skills demanded by pre-school educational programmes and that the warmth of the mother love and the fastening of children's emotional security are more important than any form of educational programme.

(Reissman, 1962) Also content that early childhood years should be utilize in firmly grounding the child in his/her subculture then exposing him/her to pre-school programmes which emphasize intellectual skills that would impose middle class values on the child and destroy the positive aspects of his/her sub culture. Also another leading scholars in early childhood education who have doubted in its wisdom are (Elkind, 1986) and (McEvoy, A., & Welker, R. , 2000). All express the fear that the short term academic gains would be offset by the long term listing of their motivation and self-initiated learning. In the same view (Stipek, D.; Feiler, R.; Daniels, D.; Milburn, S.;, 2013) cautioned that early academic gains in reading associated with formal instruction of preschoolers could' have long term negative effects on achievement.

(Robinson, 1968) in another studies in the same year have argued, that beginning early to educate children should not pose any dangers as it is difficult to see how pleasant experiences stimulating within reasonable limits and logically sequenced can be harmful to mental health or to cognitive development.

Moreover, some research evidences indicate that early childhood education have positive influences in children's effective conceptual and social development in subsequent years.

Nature, Purpose and Types of Early Child Education.

a. Nature of Pre-primary and Primary school: Pre-primary schools are in -form of kindergarten and nursery schools.
b. Nursery school or classes are places for young children usually aged 3 – 5 years which prepare them for Kindergarten class.
c. Kindergarten: Is a class or school for young children of usually 5 years which prepare them for normal school or primary education.
d. Primary: This is a school which concern with education of children between five and eleven years old, at the normal rate it has primary one to primary six i.e. a child study for good 6 years.

Purpose of Early Child Education

According to (NPE, 2013) state the following purposes of pre-primary education:

a. Providing a smooth transition from home to school.
b. Preparing the child for the primary level of education.
c. Providing adequate care and supervision for the children while their parents are at work.
d. Inculcating in the child the spirit of enquiry and creativity through the exploration of nature arid the local environment by playing with toys, artifices and musical activities etc.
e. Teaching the rudiment of numbers, letters, colours, shapes, form etc through play

f.   Inculcating social norms,

Early Detection and Identification of Children with Special Education Needs

There are two ways to detect or to find out very early these types of children:

a.   **Informal procedures**: These includes teacher rating and situational observations they are sometimes more preferable to formal procedures
b.   **Formal procedures:** This is to find out an undesirable factors in a child's development, and the child should not be a victim of inadequate teaching, malnutrition, and there should not be discontinue efforts to prevent sensory, linguistic and other problems.

Identification

Screening is the best way of identification. Screening has been implemented from neonatal period through school years. Areas considered for examination are physical, neurological, and socio-cultural and criterion referenced academic considerations.

Screening ways have been composed of various combinations of predictive tests, checklist, interviews and observations. In identification we will identify some of the target variables, such as child behaviour and other factors, and techniques used to identify and assess them e.g. choice of. Target variable classroom manifestation of learning disabilities .i.e. skills of reading, computation, handwriting and so on.

Physical behaviour i.e. general health of the child between physical and psychological, development, motor behaviour, cognitive behaviour, language behavior, social emotional behaviours.

Working With Parents (Counseling) On Continuing Work Done In School At Home

Tracking and recording information about the child at home etc. Due to their regular and intensive contact with their children, learning disabilities parents often notice early indication that their children are not learning well. A parent may therefore notice developmental lags or problems in motor, linguistic and social skills.

A survey conducted" by the California association for. Neurologically handicapped children (CANHC) indicated that mothers were often, credited with first noticing their child's problem (Tarnopol, 1977) indicated that school personnel were credited with the identification of 18% of the cases, pediatrician with 14%. The median. Age at which the problems was initially discovered. Was 4 years. However in more than 30% of the cases, the problem was not discovered until the child began attending, school.

(Bariroh, 2018) Found that some parents are not capable or willing to admit and deal with their children's learning disabilities. The various sources of information that parents usually, rely on for their screening efforts, includes comparison to sibling, information from other parents popular press and media and knowledge of behaviour expected in school.

Parent child interaction usually decide the quality of a child's early learning experiences, development of language, mental set, social attachments, and so forth. Is predicated upon intelligent, loving, support by parents (Ms. Naveena Thomas, Ms.Christy Baby, Mr. John O Pious, Ms. Cynthia Santhmayor, 2019). Parents and teacher who work actively and effectively with one another comprise a powerful team.

A productive parent professional relationship provides professionals with:
   a. Greater understanding of the. Overall needs of the child and as well as needs and desires of the parent.
   b. Data for meaningful selection of target behavior that are important to the child in her world outside the schools,
   c. Access to a wider range of social and activity reinforcement provided by parents.
   d. Increased opportunities to reinforce behaviour in both school and home settings.
   e. Feedback from parents as to Changes in behavior that, can be used to improve Programmes being implemented by professionals and parents.
   f. The ability to comply with legislation mandating continuing parental input to the educational process.

The productive parent professional relationship provides the parents with the followings:
   a. Greater understanding of the need of their child and the objectives of the teacher.
   b. Information on their rights and responsibilities as parents of an exceptional child.
   c. Specific information about their child's school program and how they can become involved.
   d. Specific ways to extend the positive effects of school programming into the home.
   e. Increased skills in helping their child learn functional behaviour that are appropriate for the home environment.
   f. Access to additional important resources (current and future) for their child.

And of most importance, a productive parent professional relationship provides the child with:
   a. Greater consistency in his/her two most important environments.
   b. Increased opportunities for learning and growth

c. Access to expanded resources and services.

Working with other professionals includes social workers, medical personnel. Their activities are normally case meetings and case conferences which is a situation in which professionals will sit and discuss the case base on observations and research findings where by minutes and papers will be written for now and future uses.

Evaluation and Assessment of Child

This is to find out the extent of the case situation on the child through test and other assessment measure and find or suggest ways of remediation of the case.

Referrals:

That is if .a measure of remediation is taken and still no positive response the child could be referred to another measures.   ,

Collaboration:

This is putting together of more than one professionals heads to attack on problem or the other in the eye of finding solutions to the problem.

In cases where a student requires support, the guidance counselor should become involved in assessing his/her needs and where necessary arrange a referral of an appropriate outside agency procedures for the referral of students to the guidance counselor and for referral to outside agencies should be include in the school plan. Psychologists provide-a source of advice to guidance counselors, on appropriate referral path-ways.

Educational Needs of Pre School Children with Special Needs

a. **Home Based Programs:**
    This largely depends on the training and cooperation of the child's parents. The parents normally assumed responsibility as

the primary care giver for their handicapped child. Parents training are usually provided by a teacher or trainer who visit the home regularly to guide the parents.

The visiting -teachers acts as a consultant and also evaluate the success of the intervention and make regular assessment of the child's progress.

In some Programmes, these home visitors (or home teachers or home advisors as they are often called) are specially trained para-professionals. They may visit as frequently as several times a week but probably no less than a few times a month in some cases they may carry the results of their assessment in home evaluation   back to other professionals who make recommendation for changes in the programme e.g. the best known home based programme is the Nationally Validated Portage Project (Karine Tremblay, 2012)

b. **Centre Based Programmes:**

In contrast to home based programs, some intervention efforts are coordinated and carried-out in a special educational setting outside the home. The setting may be part of hospital complex, a special day care center, or preschool.

In other cases children may attend a specially designed developmental center" or training center, that offers a wide range of services for children with varying types, and severities, of handicaps.

The setting can be an outdoor playground specially built that offer the combined services of many professionals and para-professionals, from several different fields. Most of these Programmes encourage social interaction and some try to integrate handicapped children with, non-handicap children in day-care or preschool classes.

In some cases the child attend the center each weekday. Sometimes for all or most of the day. And sometimes the child may come less frequently though most of the centers expect to see the child at least once a week/Parents may spends time with other professionals or take training while the child is somewhere else in the centers.

c. **Combine Home Centre Programs:**
Many programs combine the intensive help from a variety of professional in a center with the continuous attention and sensitive care from parents at time. This effort to establish intervention that carries over from center to home clearly offers many of the advantages of the two types of Programmes.

References

Bariroh, S. (2018). The Influence of Parents' Involvement on Children with Special Needs' Motivation and Learning Achievement. *International Education Studies*, Vol. 11, No. 4; 2018.

Elkind, D. (1986). *Formal Education and Early Childhood Education: An Essential Difference.* . Phi Delta Kappan, 67.

Karine Tremblay, D. L. (2012). *Assessment Of Higher Education Learning Outcomes. Feasibility Study Report Volume 1.* https://www.oecd.org/education/skills-beyond-school/AHELOFSReportVolume1.pdf.

McEvoy, A., & Welker, R. . (2000). Antisocial behavior, academic failure, and school climate a critical review. *Journal of Emotional and Behavioral disorders,*, 8(3), 130-140.

Ms. Naveena Thomas, Ms.Christy Baby, Mr. John O Pious, Ms. Cynthia Santhmayor. (2019). Parents' Awareness Of The Importance Of Parentchild Interaction For Language Development. *Global Scientific Journal* , GSJ: Volume 7, Issue 10, October 2019.

NPE, N. P. (2013). *National Policy on Education 6th Edition.* https://educatetolead.files.wordpress.com/2016/02/nationa l-education-policy-2013.pdf.

Reissman, F. (1962). *The culturally Deprived child.* New york:: Harpen.

Robinson, H. &. (1968). *The problem of timing pre-school education" in Hess, R.D and bear, R.M (Eds) Early education,* . Illiois:: Aldine publishing.

Stipek, D.; Feiler, R.; Daniels, D.; Milburn, S.;. (2013). *Effects of different instructional approaches on young children's achievement and motivation.* ISSN : 0009-3920 vol. 66.

Tarnopol, L. a. (1977). *Brain Function and Reading Disabilities.* . Baltimore: : University Park Press.

SECTION TWO:

GUIDANCE AND COUNSELING FOR LEARNERS WITH SPECIAL NEEDS.

Introduction

The place of guidance and counseling in school setting is geared towards helping students to understand self and take appropriate steps in making educational, vocational, social and psychological lifelong decisions. In addition the child's or student's welfare and the promotion, establishment and maintenance of a sound social relationship in a group is another main concern of guidance and counseling.

However, guidance and counseling can be defined separately for clarity, before, trying to see them together. According to (Parankimalil, 2015) sees guidance as assistance made available to an individual of any age by professionally qualified and adequately trained men and women to help him or her manage his/her own life and activities, develop his/her own points of view, make his/her own decision and carry his/her burdens".

Ruth Strang. "Guidance is a process of helping every individual, through his own efforts, to discover and develop his potentialities for his personal happiness and social usefulness."

A.J. Jones. "Guidance involves personal help given by a competent person; it is designed to assist a person in deciding where he wants to go, what he wants to do, or how he can best accomplish his purposes; it assists him in solving problems that arise in his life. It does not solve problems for the individual, but helps him to solve them. The focus of guidance is the individual and not the problem;

its purpose is to promote the growth of the individual in self-direction."

Knapps. "Learning about the individual student, helping him to understand himself, effecting changes in him and in his environment which will help him to grow and develop as much as possible – these are the elements of guidance."
Secondary Education Commission, 1952. "Guidance involves the difficult art of helping boys and girls to plan their own future wisely in the full light of all the factors that can be mastered about themselves and about the world in which they are to live and work."

Crow and Crow. "Guidance is assistance made available by personally and adequately trained men or women to an individual of any age to help him manage his own life activities, develop his own points of view, make his own decisions and carry his own burdens."

John Brewer. "Guidance is a process through which an individual is able to solve his problems and pursue a path suited to his abilities and aspirations."

Woodworth. "Guidance helps an individual to develop his personality and enables him to serve the society to the best of his capabilities and talents."

Kitson. "Guidance is 'individualized education'. Each student is to be helped to develop himself to the maximum possible degree in all respects."

V.M. Proctor. "Guidance is a process through which an individual or groups of individuals are helped to make necessary adjustment to the environment – inside or outside the school."

While (Paul Mupa, Tendeukai Isaac Chinooneka, 2015) sees it as a unique school function that aids to facilitate student's growth and development through intervening primarily in the non-instructional domain of school activities". It therefore can be seen as a procedure and process through which a person (Client) achieve his/her educational, vocational or personal goals.

While (Krishnan, 2020) have defined counseling as a confidential interaction between a professional and a client to achieve self-knowledge and self-direction for personal development. In the same vein (Krishnan, 2020) is of the opinion that counseling is a learning process in which individuals learn about themselves and their interpersonal relationships, thereby acquiring behavior that advance their personal development. "Counseling is a process of assisting individuals with problems or needs to solve certain adjustment problems

From the above definitions of guidance and counseling therefore, one can deduce that they are difficult to be separated as one is seen as assistance (Guidance) while the other part (counseling) is a process. Counseling services are the main aspects of guidance through which the counselor guides his client to solve his/her problems of adjustment. If guidance and counseling through which one can be help out of a problem, then the special needs person need these services more.

The special needs person no doubt has a problem of rehabilitation and adjustment. (Hartley, Susan Stuntzner and Michael T., 2014) Opined that "persons living with disabilities need psychotherapy in form of counseling to be able to be happy, effective and coherent in their life"

The Goals or Objectives of Guidance and Counseling for Special Needs Persons

i.   Fulfilling ones potential in academic achievements;
ii.   Establishing socially acceptable levels of self-care;
iii.   Developing realistic self-concepts that are in accordance with actual capacities and opportunities;

iv. Improving interpersonal relationships within the family, the school and the community;

v. Progressive in accordance with expectations in vocational self-sustenance to the degree, that is possible;

vi. Evolving a leisure life that provides major satisfactions and contributions to satisfactions of others;

vii. Assisting schools;, agencies and institutions to become more responsive to Individual's needs;

viii. Coordinating school and community resources to create a unified helping experience for the exceptional individuals, so that they may attain an optimum level of development. (Krishnan, 2020)

However, apart from the specific goals of guidance and counseling as they affect special needs persons, there are general goals of guidance and counseling that can be very relevant to the special needs persons particularly in school settings. They are:

i. Guidance and counseling equip students with the skills of making appropriate and satisfying choice.

ii. It enables students or clients develop positive self-image.

iii. It helps students develop adequate time management skills.

iv. It helps students or clients develop good inter and intra-personal relationship,

v. It helps students cope with examination anxiety.

vi. It help teachers, parents and adult members of the community, in understanding the needs and problems of their students or wards.

Other objectives as observed by (Parankimalil, 2015) are:

i. Assist the students to effect smooth translation from one educational level to the other;

ii. Encourage students to develop adaptive skills to cope with changes in family and home life.

iii. Assist school administration in improving educational opportunities and programs.

iv. Mobilize all the available resources of the school, home and community for the satisfaction of students educational, vocational and psycho-social needs.

v. Groom students for higher achievement

vi. Equip students with problem solving and decision making technique.

Scope of Counseling and Guidance

As far as guidance and counseling is concern at this level of education it is limited to four areas thus: education, vocational, social and psychological. (Pandey, 2016) has expatiate on the above areas:

1. **Educational**
   - The development of effective study skills.
   - Enhancing various bodies and facilities for placement
   - Encouraging interaction between staff and students for better understanding of each other's needs

2. **Vocational**
   - Provision of vocational information
   - Facilitate the appropriate choice of subjects

3. **Social**
   - Organizing orientation programmes for students for purpose of enlightenment
   - Development of positive interpersonal relationship among students and students, students and staffs, school and the community.
   - Encouraging good personal grooming.
   - Training in table manners
   - Provision of family and moral education.

4. **Psychological**
   - Encouraging effective time management and study habit.
   - Promoting self-worth, self-understanding.

How to Carry Out G/C to Special Needs Learners

If a normal person can be guided and counseled. It is the special need person that needs this service most for the simple fact that he is already in trouble or problems of disability. Therefore, persons without disability need to make them (disabled) understand that not all hope is lost as if one is rendered disabled in one way he/she can still make it the other, way round.

However, (Hartley, Susan Stuntzner and Michael T., 2014) has suggested counseling special need persons, particularly the disabled can be done at two basic levels, thus: the direct counseling and through the immediate society (parents, relatives, friends, school teachers etc.)

He went further to state that the first task is rehabilitating the minds of those living with disabilities. In doing this counselor should cultivate that habit of creating positive attitude towards the person with disability. Through numerous examples they should be made to understand that people living with disability have excel in some areas if given the appropriate opportunity. This apart, the client should first and foremost accept his/her disability as it enhances rehabilitating the mind.

To successfully achieve rehabilitating the mind, professional counseling skills and techniques are to be involved which include among others: empathy, reassurance, encouragement, adequate cross checking, reflection of feelings, respect for the worth and dignity of the disabled, effective verbal and nonverbal communication and also unconditional positive acceptance. With these techniques the client will understand himself well, self-disclose and accept his condition.

Furthermore, a counselor should avoid the mistake of giving false re-assurance to the client as there may be lack of confident on the counselor. Another important point here that is worthy of mention is the use of team approach in guidance and counseling. A part from the professional counselors, there should be, other professionals such as: pediatricians, psychologist, social workers, nutritionists, speech and hearing therapists, ophthalmologists etc. According to (Hartley, Susan Stuntzner and Michael T., 2014) the counselors should be able to provide usable information to the client in the following critical and important areas.

Guidance Needs of Learners with Special Needs

With the recent coming of the inclusive education formally referred as integration is not sufficient to address the needs so long as they are not valued and respected. They need to have that sense of worthiness and capable of doing it if given necessary support, so as to develop "a success identify"

(Fuandai, 2010) Observed that the exceptional children (Special Needs) need to be trained to develop a successful identify, that is they need to view themselves as successful capable, and as persons valued as an individual.

He continue that the "disables and handicapped children need to experience success as it applies to all children" These are categories of people that have experienced failure for quite a long time in their life, therefore, there is need to re-assure them that success on their part is possible. So, whatever inspiration and interest one has to a special need person towards his success had to be genuine. In addition to the above measures, the special need person can consciously made to lead to interact with peers with social gathering as this could be factors that enhance success experience for the young special need person. The special need people should be encouraged not to pity, as it tells little about a person. (Fuandai, 2010) Agree to this assertion where he stated the traditional reaction of pity that disability and handicapped individuals often elicit in others, is not helpful or constructive, in that it implies minimal expectations.

He further stress that "this attitude also, consequently conveys negative message that persons living with disability is not thought to be capable or worthy of successful achievement".

However, the special needs person have motivational needs just as a normal person. The highest basic needs required by an individual propounded by Abraham Maslow 1954 (Saul Mcleod, 2023) is self – Actualization needs which is a stage of being self-satisfied or self-fulfilled or self-containment of course the special need persons need to be self fulfilled, self contained etc. as humans. Therefore, the remaining four can be applied too they are:

- **1st Stage: Physiological Needs**
  It is all about satisfaction of human and thirst. They can eat and doing so as to survive.
- **2nd Stage: Safety Need**
  When security orderliness and stability are needed. They need safety where ever they are.
- **3rd state – Blending and love needed**
  This involves affection love and identification. The special need person needs love and care which come through identification. He need have sense of belongings which will make him feel high place and accommodated.
- **4th stage: Esteem Needs**
  Here one experience prestige, highly places and respect. Other needs of learner with specials needs may include: Health, vocational, educational, Job and career, family relationship e.t.c.

Clues on How to Counsel Special Need Persons or Students

(Santrock, 2006) Offered the following counseling suggestions for teachers working with students living with disabilities:

- Carry out each child's individualized education plan (IEP)
- Use the support that is available and seek other support. Many specialists in the community might be willing to help to help or be consulted.
- Encourage the school to provide increased support and training on how to teach children with special needs.
- Become more knowledgeable about the type of special needs students in the class. Read educational journals and books.
- Avoid labeling a student with a disability.
- Established a good relationship with students with special needs, which include: Be caring, accepting and patient, have positive expectation for learning, help student with their social and communication skills as well as academic, plan and organize the classroom effectively be enthusiastic and help students become motivated to learn, monitor children learning and provide effective feedback.
- Help children without disability to understand and accept children with disabilities, children without special needs should be given adequate information about children with special needs. There should be opportunities for both students to interact through peer tutoring and group learning activities can be used to encourage interactions among students.
- The teacher should keep up to date on the ICT that is available for educating children with special needs.

In a related development on conditions of counseling special needs persons and their families, (Oluremi, 2015)) suggested the following principles:

a. The counselor must know himself by having an accurate insight into his personality and how it will affects his counseling practice.
b. The counsellor must possess a certain body of knowledge and must be above and beyond competency in general counseling principles and techniques.
c. The counsellor must possess certain attitude. This attitude must be positive about disabilities and their treatment or management. He must be free from stereotypes and have positive attitude towards individuals with disabilities and their families.
d. The counsellor must exhibit positive counseling behaviour and attitudes. These behaviour and attitudes include empathy respect, positive regard, and warmth, genuine towards his clients.
e. The counsellor must be able to develop good counseling relationships. The counsellor should establish rapport with the client so that they can work together to achieve desirable results. The client's needs must always be given first consideration, not counselor's preference.
f. The   counsellor must appreciate and recognized individual differences. Individual clients are different, have different problems and will need different kinds of assistance.
g. The counseling environment should be non-threatening. The physical and psychological environment should be generally comfortable. There should be good lighting, ventilation, cleanliness, well arranged, good furniture, privacy, freedom from distractions   and interruption.
h. The counsellor must see the counseling should be open as learning process for both client and counsellor, etc. ,

Qualities of A Good Counsellor to Special Needs Persons

The major function of a counsellor to the special need person is to help him or her deal with personal problems and make decision about the course his or her life should take. Since counselors are individuals, it is therefore inevitable that they can vary as to the importance they attach to their counseling roles.

Consequently there are certain qualities that the Special Needs Person in particular appreciates most, they are confidence and empathy then others follows. This assertion is in total agreement with what (Oluremi, 2015) said "Specialist counselors must demonstrate confidence more readily than others, exhibit empathy and patience in their relationships with disabled and handicapped children".

He continued to note that:

In this regard, the disabled and handicapped children will feel they can talk to them, and trust their two qualities: EMPATHY and CONFIDENCE (trust worthiness), rather than any great familiarity with counseling techniques, that disabled and handicapped children appear to look for, when deciding to whom they should turn to, when in need.

However, other factors or qualities that can make a good counsellor may include:

a. Respect
b. Caring
c. Forgiveness
d. Loyalty
e. Cooperation
f. Shared interests
g. Affection
h. Trust
i. Honesty
j. Sharing information
k. Exchanging gifts
l. Visiting each other's family
m. Giving support in times of trouble and
n. Happiness

o.   Making positive comments about each other etc.

Counseling the Special Needs Persons through Parents, Relatives, Friends and School Staff

Without doubt these categories of people need to counselled the Special Needs individuals more particularly the parents, for no other reason than their togetherness. This apart, according to (Fuandai, 2010) "parent's feel the immediate pinged of their child's handicap because the immediate needs of the child are tied on them.

(Bariroh, 2018) is of the opinion that, Most parents of children with special need do not know the features of their disabled children neither, do they have any idea of what to think about, concerning the future of their disabled children. They cannot project what the future has in store for their wards, they crop up from time to time. It is the role of the counselor to explain to them where they can get the best educational programmes for the child.

With this scenario parents can experience disruption, stress, anxiety bitterness trauma etc. they therefore, need proper counseling by a professional so as to cope with the situation and pick courage to face the challenges ahead. (Oluremi, 2015) has enumerated reasons why parents or families of special needs counseling which can equally be applicable to relatives, school staff and others thus:

a.   To accept, love and care for the handicapped child.
b.   To help adjust in the society and to reduce their negative reactions towards the child and others.
c.   To help them look for scientific solutions to their problems
d.   To keep them away from superstitious belief and to correct their misconceptions about the causes of handicapped
e.   To help them know the causes and prevention of handicaps in children or avoiding future occurrence.
f.   To help plan their budget in such a way that either members of the family will not suffer.

g.   To help them know agencies and organizations that provide education, diagnosis, employment, special equipment, special education and even financial assistance.
h.   To help them known and understand various behavior and ways by which handicapped children learn.
i.   To help them develop personal effectiveness to overcome obstacles in the way of progress etc.

The parents, relatives etc. can make use of the above mentioned points to see reason for having positive attitudes toward persons with special needs as well as counsel them. By counseling them their degree of problems will greatly be reduced. In trying to counsel parents it is imperative to note:

a.   Presentation of information on child's disability as it relates to factor that affect the child's learning potentials
b.   The development of a realistic supportive education plan within the school.
c.   Offering support to the parents in dealing with their feelings related to the problems associated with the handicap.
d.   Teaching parents to enhance their general understanding and acceptance of the disability the child is suffering from,
e.   Teaching parents about strategies of behavior management

Counseling Needs Of Families with Special Needs Learners

Family counseling is a "therapeutic technique for exploring and attempting to alleviate the present interlocking emotional and other related problems within a given family system in the effort to remediate the concern faced by one of the family, while (Krishnan, 2020) see family counseling as " a process through which members of the family are rendered assistance designed with one another and to develop a better understanding of the conditions within which they live"

There is great need for families of special need persons to be counseled for the fact that disability or exceptionality is welcome in most families with negative reactions which result to other problems. The most common reactions of families of special need according to (Fuandai, 2010):

a. **Rejection:** The rejection can be directed toward the child, the medical doctor or nurse or any members of the family who may be accused of causing the misfortune. The worse form of rejection is a "death wish" for the child.
b. **Denial:** A denial that the condition of the child is not true or that the child is growing through normal development process. The notion is always that such a handicapped child cannot be in the family.
c. **Overprotection:** Usually demonstrated by not allowing the child to move or explore within his environment. The child may be secluded from other children and kept in a separate place for fear that he is pruned to danger.

In the same vein (Bariroh, 2018) also observed the following reactions among parents of handicapped children.

a. **Loss of self-esteem:** they perceive the child as refection of their in adequacies and imperfections.
b. **Feeling of share and guilt:** parents may blame themselves if they think they are responsible or contribute to making the child a handicapped. This is more so when they were careless or they refuse to carry out medical advice or instruction.
c. **Feeling of defensiveness:** defending the child as not having a real handicap, or interpreting it to be temporary or not a handicap at all.
d. **Self-reproach:** Being sorry for being a cause of somehow
e. **Self-sacrifice:** some parents would prefer to die rather than seeing the child exist as a handicapped or they prefer to die if the child came back to normally etc.

In the same vain fear is another reaction from parent and family members when a question that has no immediate answers may arise, for instance, can the child attend school? What will happen to the child when he has grown up? Etc.

(Krishnan, 2020) Said on common reactions of parents of special needs children that People often fear the unknown more than they fear the known. Having the complete diagnosis and some knowledge of the children future prospects can be easier than uncertainty. In either case, however, fear of the future is the emotion: what is going to happen to this child when he is five years old, when he is twelve, when is twenty-one?

They continue to say that there is also fear of society's rejection, fears about how brothers and sisters will be affected, and questions as to whether there will be any more brothers or sisters in this family and concerns about whether the husband or wife will love this child.

Another reaction worth mentioning is confusion as the period is very tense. Many, parents may not fully understand what will follow thereafter. This of cause can result to sleepless night and not being able to make decision.

Parent could become traumatized, disturbed and uncertain, about whatever new information received. (Hartley, Susan Stuntzner and Michael T., 2014). Are of the view that parent become more confused when they hear new medical terminologies that describes something they do not understand.

The Counseling Needs

(Agomoh O E and Atteng C J , 2011) have noted that parents of special need persons need the following types of counseling

a. **Information counseling:**
    Here parents are provided with information in some of the following areas.

i. Information on agencies and organizations that deal with the handicapped
ii. Counselor services
iii. Causes and prevention of handicaps
iv. Employment for the handicapped
v. Evaluation and diagnosis
vi. Referrals and placement
vii. Educational services
viii. Special equipment
ix. Appraisals
x. Follow up or after care service

b. Adjustment Counseling
i. To avoid blame
ii. Seek for scientific solutions
iii. To cope with the problems imposed the child
iv. Absorb social stigma
v. Accept, love and care for the child
vi. remove fear, anxiety guilt etc
vii. Genetic Counseling
viii. care of pregnancy
ix. prevention of handicaps
x. causes of handicaps due to
xi. Misuse of drugs
xii. Malnutrition
xiii. Genetic abnormalities etc

c. Reality Counseling
i. To accept that the child is handicapped
ii. That the child will live with the handicap
iii. That they (parents) will have to provide certain basic necessities
iv. That the child will do well when he has the necessary provisions

v.   That the cause of the handicap is a reality and has a scientific basis

vi.   That only scientific solution will be sought to help both parents and the child.

d. Taking away the mental pain

i.   Give examples of similar causes closer home and even far away   of other parents problems

ii.   Give individual and group counseling were appropriate

iii. How to teach some specific skills

iv.   Direct them to source of help or support (if any)

e. . Community Involvement

The best way community can become involved in counseling the special need person is through the use of community education. According to Flatcher (1980) in Danesy A (2008) defined community members to the education of its citizens through participating development of the less privilege members such as the vulnerable children, person with disabilities and so on.

While Menzey and Le Tarte (1972) in Dansey a (2008) looks at community education as philosophical concept which served the entire community members. Going by the above definitions communities expect to become involve in all aspects of development, counseling included.

References

Agomoh O E and Atteng C J . (2011). Counseling Teachers for Excellent Academic Performance of Students with special needs in Nigeria the special educator. *The journal of Nigeria association of special education teachers (NASET)* , Vol 10 No.1.

Bariroh, S. (2018). The Influence of Parents' Involvement on Children with Special Needs' Motivation and Learning Achievement. *International Education Studies*, Vol. 11, No. 4; 2018.

Fuandai, C. M. (2010). Catering For Children With Special Needs In The Regular Classroom: Challenges And The Way Forward. *Edo Journal of Counselling*, Vol. 3, No. 1,.

Hartley, Susan Stuntzner and Michael T. (2014). Disability and the Counseling Relationship: What Counselors Need to Know. *American Counseling Association Conference,.* https://www.counseling.org/docs/default-source/vistas/article_09.pdf.

Krishnan, S. (2020). *Counseling and Consultancy Psychology* . India: Department of Psychology, University college Kerala University .

Ms. Naveena Thomas, Ms.Christy Baby, Mr. John O Pious, Ms. Cynthia Santhmayor. (2019). Parents' Awareness Of The Importance Of Parentchild Interaction For Language Development. *Global Scientific Journal* , GSJ: Volume 7, Issue 10, October 2019.

NPE, N. P. (2013). *National Policy on Education 6th Edition.* https://educatetolead.files.wordpress.com/2016/02/national-education-policy-2013.pdf.

Oluremi, D. (2015). Counselling Intervention and Support Programmes for Families. *Journal of Education and Practice*, Vol.6, No.10, 2015.

Pandey, D. S. (2016). *Guidance and Counseling in Education.* New Delhi : VIKAS Publishing House PVT LTD .

Parankimalil, J. (2015). *Meaning and Definition of Guidance.* https://johnparankimalil.wordpress.com/2015/01/16/meaning-and-definition-of-guidance/.

Santrock, J. (2006). *Educational Psychology and Classroom: .* Update New York.: MC Graw Hill.

Saul Mcleod. (2023). *Maslow's Hierarchy Of Needs (1954).* https://simplypsychology.org/maslow.html.

Stipek, D.; Feiler, R.; Daniels, D.; Milburn, S.;. (2013). *Effects of different instructional approaches on young children's achievement and motivation.* ISSN : 0009-3920 vol. 66.

Tarnopol, L. a. (1977). *Brain Function and Reading Disabilities. .* Baltimore: : University Park Press.

SECTION THREE:

INFORMATION COMMUNICATION TECHNOLOGY ICT FOR LEARNERS WITH SPECIAL NEEDS

What is Information Technology?

Information Technology (IT) is the study or use of electronic devices, especially computers for processing, analyzing, storing, and sending out information. In addition, the Oxford Advanced Learners Dictionary states that, Communication is a method of sending information, especially through telephones, radio, and computers etc. Therefore, Information and Communication Technology refers to the use of electronic devices, especially computers in processing, analyzing, storing and sending out information. It can be applied to the education of special need children and normal children alike.

Information:

The term Information can be refers to as news passed to you either orally or written for example "it will be rainy tomorrow", it does not matter whether they are true or false. The story being passed to you is known as information if the information given to you is true then it is said to be fact. Information is data which has been processed in such a way to be meaningful and useful to the person that receives.

Information and communications technology (ICT) is often used as an extended synonym for information technology (IT), but is a more specific term that stresses the role of unified communications and the integration of telecommunications (telephone lines and wireless signals), computers as well as necessary enterprise software, middleware, storage, and audio-visual systems, which enable users to access, store, transmit, and manipulate information.

The term ICT is also used to refer to the convergence of audio-visual and telephone networks with computer networks through a single cabling or link system. There are large economic incentives (huge cost savings due to elimination of the telephone network) to merge the telephone network with the computer network system using a single unified system of cabling, signal distribution and management.

Information Technology (IT) is the application of computers and telecommunications equipment to store, retrieve, transmit and manipulate data, often in the context of a business or other enterprise. The term is commonly used as a synonym for computers and computer networks, but it also encompasses other information distribution technologies such as television and telephones. Several industries are associated with information technology, including computer hardware, software, electronics, semiconductors, internet, telecom equipment, e-commerce and computer services

Humans have been storing, retrieving, manipulating and communicating information since the Sumerians in Mesopotamia developed writing in about 3000 BC, but the term information technology in its modern sense first appeared in a 1958 article published in the Harvard Business Review; authors Harold J. Leavitt and Thomas L. Whistler commented that "the new technology does not yet have a single established name. We shall call it information technology (IT)." Their definition consists of three categories: techniques for processing, the application of statistical and mathematical methods to decision-making, and the simulation of higher-order thinking through computer programs.

Based on the storage and processing technologies employed, it is possible to distinguish four distinct phases of IT development: pre-mechanical (3000 BC – 1450 AD), mechanical (1450–1840), electromechanical (1840–1940) and electronic (1940–present)

Computer

A computer is a general purpose device that can be programmed to carry out a set of arithmetic or logical operations automatically. Since a sequence of operations can be readily changed, the computer can solve more than one kind of problem. Computer can be define as an electronic device (hardware) capable of accepting data (input) storing it producing information (output) through set of instruction by the user latter Programme (software).

Hardware: can be referred to as physical component that can be seen and touched with our hands.

Software: can be refer to as the interchangeable part of computer that cannot be seen or touch with your hands

Input: can be refer to as the part of the computer that the user insert data into the computer for processing. It can also be seen as events, activities, and transaction that have been recorded, it is the raw material from which information is produced e.g. joystick, scanner.

Output: can be refer to as the device that help computer to send out the outcome of process or analysis data they include monitors, speak.

System: can be referred to interdependence and interrelated parts and function such that the activity of one will affect the general operation for example then body computer system.

Conventionally, a computer consists of at least one processing element, typically a central processing unit (CPU), and some form of memory. The processing element carries out arithmetic and logic operations, and a sequencing and control unit can change the order of operations in response to stored information. Peripheral devices allow information to be retrieved from an external source, and the result of operations saved and retrieved.

In World War II, mechanical analog computers were used for specialized military applications. During this time the first electronic digital computers were developed. Originally they were the size of a large room, consuming as much power as several hundred modern personal computers (PCs).

Modern computers based on integrated circuits are millions to billions of times more capable than the early machines, and occupy a fraction of the space. Simple computers are small enough to fit into mobile devices, and mobile computers can be powered by small batteries. Personal computers in their various forms are icons of the Information Age and are what most people think of as "computers." However, the embedded computers found in many devices from MP3 players to fighter aircraft and from toys to industrial robots are the most numerous.

History of computer technology
Devices have been used to aid computation for thousands of years, probably initially in the form of a tally stick. The Antikythera mechanism, dating from about the beginning of the first century BC, is generally considered to be the earliest known mechanical analog computer, and the earliest known geared mechanism. Comparable geared devices did not emerge in Europe until the 16th century, and it was not until 1645 that the first mechanical calculator capable of performing the four basic arithmetical operations was developed.

Generation is the gradual development of computer that is how that computer came into existence generation means the historical development of computer starting from the use of abacus, the first generation to fifth generation of computer s ABACUS 450BC it is a warden frame containing rod with small ball that slide along them. It the first machine that was used to display data, it was used as a tool for counting.

First Generation of Computer (1940s-1950s)
The first generation are the type of computers that are very large in a large and make use of mechanical language in their programme, they seen as difficult to understand and use. The make use of vacuum as their memory device for keeping and storing device e.g. Universal automatic computer (UNIVAC)

Characteristics

-        Use of mechanical language

-        Low memory capacity

-        Lot of noise and large in size

-        Generate lot of heat

-        Slow in operation

Second Generation of Computer (1950s-1960s)
There was reduction in everything from the first one the trial of changing the mechanical language was not successful of that level. They make use of transistor for keeping and storing of data e.g Atlas

Characteristics

-        Use of human readable language

-        Increase in memory capacity

-        Easy to acquire and maintain

-        Less noise and heat

-        Size become small]

Third Generation of Computer (1960s-1970s)
This is the period when the mechanical language used by computer was converted to low level language or human readable language. It is also the beginning of the modern day computer here integrate

circuit was used as the memory device for storing and keeping of data. e.g. ICL 1900 series.

Characteristics

-        Easy to acquire and maintain

-        Use of human readable language

-        Memory capacity was increased

-        Less noise and heat

-        Fast in operation

Fourth Generation of Computer (1970s-1980s)
They were design with the ability to carry out human and artificial intelligent Programme to increase the speed and keeping of data e.g. palm top.

Characteristics

-        More friendly and cheaper

-        Fast in operation

-        Small and portable

-        Less heat and noise

-        Increase in memory capacity

Fifth Generation of Computer (1980s-1990s)
This is the generation that exists up to date; device used in this generation is called micro cheap. Here computer can perform human and artificial Programme meaning that they are predictable and also be used of network e.g. Robot.

Characteristic

-        They are portable (smaller in size)

-        Increase in memory capacity

-        Fast and accurate

-        No noise

Electronic computers, using either relays or valves, began to appear in the early 1940s. The electromechanical Zuse Z3, completed in 1941, was the world's first programmable computer, and by modern standards one of the first machines that could be considered a complete computing machine. Colossus, developed during the Second World War to decrypt German messages was the first electronic digital computer. Although it was programmable, it was not general-purpose, being designed to perform only a single task. It also lacked the ability to store its program in memory; programming was carried out using plugs and switches to alter the internal wiring.[The first recognizably modern electronic digital stored-program computer was the Manchester Small-Scale Experimental Machine (SSEM), which ran its first program on 21 June 1948.

The development of transistors in the late 1940s at Bell Laboratories allowed a new generation of computers to be designed with greatly reduced power consumption. The first commercially available stored-program computer, the Ferranti Mark I, contained 4050 valves and had a power consumption of 25 kilowatts. By comparison the first transistorized computer, developed at the University of Manchester and operational by November 1953, consumed only 150 watts in its final version.

IBM introduced the first hard disk drive in 1956, as a component of their 305 RAMAC computer system. Most digital data today is still stored magnetically on hard disks, or optically on media such as CD-ROMs. Until 2002 most information was stored on analog devices, but that year digital storage capacity exceeded analog for the first time. As of 2007 almost 94% of the data stored worldwide was held digitally: 52% on hard disks, 28% on optical devices and

11% on digital magnetic tape. It has been estimated that the worldwide capacity to store information on electronic devices grew from less than 3 Exabyte's in 1986 to 295 Exabyte's in 2007 doubling roughly every 3 years.

The Role of Information and Communication Technology

Information is a fundamental commodity. It is through the discovery of new information, its dissemination and sharing that society advances.

Information and communication technology is concerned with imparting of information not just simple acquisition of declarative facts, but also procedural information such as how to do things, how to learn. A vital recent development in the ICT is the convergence of technology concerned with the processing of information with that which deals mainly with its communication. This is clearly seen in the emergence of the internet whereby the processing power in each office and school can be connected and communicated with corresponding system anywhere in the world.

It should not be forgotten that ICT is part of the curriculum in all developed countries.

Need for Communication and Information

Every student in school needs some method of communication in order to interact with others and learn from social contact. Students who are nonverbal or whose speech is not fluent or understandable enough to communicate effectively may benefit from using some type of communication device or devices. Communication devices include such things as symbol systems, communication boards and wallets, programmable switches, electronic communication devices, speech synthesizers, recorded speech devices, communication enhancement software, and voiced word processing. Assistive Listening much of the time in school, students are expected to learn through listening. Students who have hearing impairments or auditory processing problems can be at a distinct disadvantage unless they learn to use the hearing they have. or they develop alternative means for getting information.

I C T for persons with hearing problems

Hearing problems may be progressive, permanent, or intermittent. Any of these impairments may interfere significantly with learning to speak, read, and follow directions.

Assistive devices to help with hearing and auditory processing problems include: hearing aids, personal FM units, sound field FM systems, Phonic Ear, TDDs, or closed caption TV (Cook. A. M. & Hussey S M. , 1995)

ICT for Persons with Visual Problems

Visual Aids. Vision is also a major learning mode. General methods for assisting with vision problems include increasing contrast, enlarging stimuli and making use of tactile and auditory models. Devices that assist with vision include screen readers, screen enlargers. Magnifiers, large-type books, taped books, Braillers, light boxes, high contrast materials. thermoform graphics, synthesizers, and scanners.

Mobility. Individuals whose physical impairments limit their mobility may need any of a number of devices to help them get around in the school building and participate in student activities. Mobility devices include such things as self-propelled walkers, manual or powered wheelchairs, and powered recreational vehicles like bikes and scooters.

Computer-Based Instruction

Computer-based instruction can make possible independent participation in activities related to the curriculum. Software can be selected which mirrors the conceptual framework of the regular curriculum. but offers an alternative way of responding to exercises and learning activities. Software can provide the tools for written expression, spelling, calculation, reading, basic reasoning, and higher level thinking skills. The computer can also be used to access a wide variety of databases.

Social Interaction and Recreation

Students with disabilities want to have fun and interact socially with their peers. Assistive technology can help them to participate in all sorts of recreational activities which can be in interactive with friends. Some adapted recreational activities include drawing software, computer games, computer simulations, painting with a head or mouth wand, interactive laser disks, and adapted puzzles.

Importance of ICT in Special Needs Education

Be realistic about your child's capabilities and needs. Information technology can open up exciting new opportunities for a child, but it is not magic. There are certain basic requirements for any individual to be successful with technology, and it is important to face these requirements squarely. There is nothing more disappointing or discouraging than purchasing expensive equipment for a child which is beyond his or her capabilities to use.

Prerequisites for Computer Use

Physical or sensory impairments do not limit access to computers, but cognition is a factor in computer operation. The major prerequisite for using a computer (with or without adaptations) is the cognitive ability to understand cause and effect. The child must be able to understand that the computer operates (e.g., changes, does something) because the child has activated the equipment through some volitional movement or activity (e.g., eyebeam, speaking, puffing into a straw, hitting a switch). Some children enjoy playing with switches by hitting them randomly but may not be able to connect their own behavior to the response their movement activates. In order to be successful in interacting with a computer, the user must be able to control some volitional activity and to do so consistently. For example, the child would have to be able to activate the computer in response to a visual, tactile, or auditory prompt. Another prerequisite to computer use is the ability to make conscious, meaningful choices between alternatives like yes and no. The choices can be very simple ones, but there has' to be evidence that the child has made an actual decision and not merely acted randomly. If a child does not have the concept of cause and effect or cannot make consistent choices, using a computer is probably not a worthwhile next step at this point in the child's development.

The Educational Uses of Information and Communication Technology

Computer Programmes can be used to teach the students directly It has a number of benefits, as it often requires a kind of individual attention of the learner. It is particularly useful in drill and practice lessons, where repetition is necessary in order for concept of skill to be learned. This can be most useful to children with learning disabilities. When interacting with machine, there is no danger of annoying or upsetting another person, no matter how many times the drill and practice is done.

The use of Information and Communication Technology in Teaching the Deaf.

1. Enhances language improvement of deaf people through constant exposure to reading and retrieval of information system.
2. Improves grammar, spelling and overall sentence construction of deaf people since more time is spent on the screen with language tasks.
3. Encourages individualized instruction, which permits exploration, experimentation and self-discovery.
4. Exposes students to different texts of language variation used by people in the deaf child's immediate and far away environment, and provides exposure to learning processes, which cannot take place in the classroom situation alone.

Computer technology enables deaf people to express themselves and help the surrounding hearing people understand the deaf individual's thinking process, feelings and need (Edwards, 1995)

The use of information and communication technology has come to stay. Further research will be necessary to determine its effects on the education of deaf children.

ICT for Distance Learning

ICT can be used as part of distance teaching tool. This will be effective when (specialized) teachers are short in supply and "nave to be shared between geographically dispersed students and teachers.

Communication can take place in different modes and requires different rates of information. This can be done with the use of internet, below is a description of how the internet works.

ICT can also form a useful communication medium between people with different sensory abilities. (Coombs, 1995) Shows how a blind teacher may be able to communicate with a deaf student despite their mismatch of abilities; thanks to email, and modern communication equipment's, like the tablet phones IPad, blackberry etc.

While e-mail is normally used for communication between distant locations, it can be used as a means of local face-to-face communication.

The World Wide Web (www) is a particular form of communication, which has rapidly gained importance such that it is almost becoming an inevitable information source, not the least in education

The Implementation (MAKING IT REALITY)

There are a number of points that have to be considered if the introduction and maintenance of ICT in special education is to be successful.

i.   The need to train teachers well. While it may seem expensive to acquire the equipment, there will be no need buying them when there are no qualified teachers to operate them. Therefore it will only be adopted if the people who might use it are confident in its use and convinced of its usefulness.

ii.   There is a need for supportive staff to maintain and repair the equipment.

iii.   Constant monitoring at all levels is also vital. This applies to Programmes of ICT use, so that the job is not over when the equipment had been obtained and teachers have been trained. They should not be simply left to get on with it but should be supported and monitored. As they develop and learn, and as the technology also improves, there should be re-assessment and updating.

References

Cook. A. M. & Hussey S M. . (1995). *Assistive technologies: Principles and practice,*. Sl. LOUIs: : Mosby. .

Coombs, N. (1995). *Interfacing online services Alternative Inputs, and redundant dis; York:, J:ays. In A. 0 N. Edwards (Ed). Extra- ordinary human computer interaction.* New York: Cambridge University Press.

Edwards, A. D. (1995). *Computers and people with disabilities. In Edwards (Ed) Extra-ordinary human computer interaction.* New York : Cambridge University Press, pp. 19-44.

Elkind, D. (1986). *Formal Education and Early Childhood Education: An Essential Difference.* . Phi Delta Kappan, 67.

SECTION FOUR:

REHABILITATION

Introduction

The term Rehabilitation has several definition given by several scholars from different field based on their individual perception and understanding. It can be defined as the restoration of someone to a useful place in the society.

In medical approach, Rehabilitation is described as specialized healthcare dedicated to improving or restoring physical strength etc. It can also be referred to as the restoration of the handicapped person to the fullest physical, mental, vocational and economic usefulness of which they are capable.

It can also be defined as any process that seeks to restore a patient to a previous Level of health education, social and economic usefulness.

Rehabilitation aimed at enabling the disabled person to reach and maintain their physical, sensory, intellectual, psychological and social functional levels. Rehabilitation provides disabled people with the tools they need to attain independence and self-determination.

(Govindan, 2010) Rehabilitation is punishment based on the psychology and sociology of crime. The goal of rehabilitation is to return the offender to society neither embittered nor resolved to get even for his degradation and suffering, but possessing a new set of values and morals and a desire to contribute to society. Rehabilitation is a process of helping a non-productive or deviant person towards restoration or the desired standards.

Rehabilitation is the process of training the disabled individuals about a certain skills which will enable them become self-sufficient, self-determined and self-reliant.

Difference between Rehabilitation and Habitation

Rehabilitation is simply a way of training the handicapped person who have acquired disabilities or handicap after their birth or at their later life. It is a Specialized training tailored for handicapped who have already a certain skills before they become handicapped as a result of accident or disease in their later life.

While, Habitation can simply refers to some specialized training process or Programme for disable person who have sustained their dis-abilities Right from birth or before they could acquire any skills or vocation.

Rehabilitation is also looked as combined and coordinated use of medical, social, educational, and vocational measures for an individual to attain the highest possible level of functional ability. Rehabilitation is a planned orderly sequence of services related to the total needs of the handicapped individual and the attempt of a vocational Rehabilitation counselor to help solve these vocational problems and this brings about vocational adjustment of the handicapped individual. (Kostelink, M.J., Whiren. A.P., Soderman, A.K. & Gregory, K. , 2006)

The goal of rehabilitation is helping the individual to be fully adjusted to the norms of his group and society.

Disability is a condition, which is not a respecter of person in that it can occur at any time in the life of an individual. Disability effects individual of diverse race, age, religion affiliation, and social class. When disability strikes, no matter the time or age of an onset or the type of the disability, the individual is usually relatively affected as a condition the individual needs adjust to the condition and help him/herself to function and be productive to a certain extend the disability can allow. The individuals with disabilities, whether children youth, adults, or elderly need one form of Rehabilitation Programme or the other, in order to be independent of him/herself and productive.

Disability can basically be classified into two.

- Physical Disabilities and
- Psychological Disabilities.

Types of Rehabilitation
Rehabilitation could be classified broadly as.

a. Educational Rehabilitation.
b. Vocational Rehabilitation.
c. Medical Rehabilitation.
d. Psycho-social Rehabilitation.

Educational Rehabilitation

Educational Rehabilitation is achieved through Special education is first recognized 2004 edition process of Rehabilitation; event through medical Rehabilitation had existed since medical age of the existence of disability.

The definitions of Special Education are many and the following are some of them.

Special education is defined as "an area within a frame work of general Education that provides",

i.   Appropriate facilities
ii.   Specialized materials and methods, and
iii.   Teachers with Special training, for children considered handicapped (Kostelink, M.J., Whiren. A.P., Soderman, A.K. & Gregory, K. , 2006)

Special Education is a form of Education of children and adult who have learning difficulty because of different sort of handicapped; blindness, partial sightedness, deafness, hardness of hearing, mental retardation etc. Due to circumstances of birth, inheritance, social position, mental and physical health pattern, or accident in later life.

Harward and Orlansky (1980) defined special education as "The individually, planned, and systematically monitored arrangement of physical settings of special equipment and materials, teaching procedure and other interventions designed to help exceptional children achieve the greater possible self-sufficient and academic success. "

Olubela (2000),"asserts special education greatly. Emphasizes cognitive development of persons with disabilities. It also makes provisions (in its curriculum) for the development of the effective and psychomotor domains of man as posited by Bloom in his Taxonomy of Education objectives".

The federal government Programme of education for all (EFA) emphasizes equal education for all person their disabilities or their handicap pic condition notwithstanding.

Therefore all the handicapped studying special or any other course of study either in the segregation setting mainstreaming education Rehabilitation .

Vocational Rehabilitation
Vocational Rehabilitation is that type of education that exposes learners or handicapped to a particular skills which will help them become self-sufficient and self-reliant. It refers to all concerted effort at equipping the individual with needful skills at functional productively on a vocation of choice. A vocation is a job which one does for a living; for a giving service to others as needed. It also refers to as employment one engage into be in keeping with the economic demands. Vocational Rehabilitation could be provided for the disabled in:

a. Institutional setting e.g. Technical schools and colleges of technology.
b. Special vocational Rehabilitation centers.
c. Sheltered workshops.
d. On-the-job vocational training centers.
e. Community Based vocational Rehabilitation centers. (CBVR).

Special Vocational Rehabilitation Centers

Vocational Rehabilitation centers are established by the government and other Non-Governmental Organizations (NGO's) to train the disabled individuals in typing, cloth weaving, woodworks, Textile design, carpentry, tie and Dying, Leatherwork, Mat making, Weaving Brick, laying, Brick/block making, Tailoring, Basket making Soap-making Home economics, Poultry keeping, and Animal Husbandry. Etcetera.

Medication Rehabilitation

Medical Rehabilitation refers to the services that are provided or rendered by medical profession to help persons with disabilities to maximize the residual abilities. This involves the dispensing of drugs therapy to the individual with disabilities through the various hospitals, health centers, medical homes delivery as well as mobile health care services.

Medical rehabilitation aims at preventing disabilities, restoring loss abilities and developing functional abilities. Medical Rehabilitation is diagnostic, preventive and curative in practice.

Stages of Medical Rehabilitation

i. **Preventive Rehabilitation:** This include primary health services e.g. anti-polio vaccination, immunization and awareness education in the prevention of disease as river blindness, measles, and polio misdates. Etc.

ii.   **Early medical Rehabilitation stage:** This is done in order to prevent the severity of disabilities. It can also reduce the pains, and accelerate returns of the victim to normal living.

iii.   **Late medical Rehabilitation stage:** This is earning out in special education institution or vocational Rehabilitation centers in order to train the handicap become useful to them self and the society.

Professional In Medical Field: They include: Ophthalmologist, optician, dentist, otolaryngologist, physiotherapy, Audiologist, cynclologist, orthopedic, psychiatrists. etc.

Psychosocial Rehabilitation

This is the heart of Rehabilitation. It facilitate functional, social integration, which is the ultimate goal of rehabilitation. This is because the ability of an individual to live adequately in the ever dynamic society largely depends on his ability to psychologically as per with his counterparts in the society (Olubela 2000; 2002) He asserts that various experience reveal that many individual with disabilities who had undergone one form of educational, medical or and vocational into their society, she observed that "when client are initially registered in rehabilitation centers they feel dejected and behave as if hope is lost. When Rehabilitation programme commences the individual "pick up hope thus they become responsive to services.

Wanock (1978) said "people with special needs are often unemployed or underemployed simply because they are not provided with the right help at the right time even when they were employed they experienced discrimination, stereotype and mockery by their co-workers.

Therefore unless psychosocial Rehabilitation rendered that the disabled individual will be able to cope with their training in the rehabilitation centers and also overcome all their disabilities or handicapped condition. The disable need to be given freedom to exercise his civil rights as the non-disabled counterparts, he need to marry and be married; they needs to be independent productive citizen. Olubela (2002) submitted that getting the disabled on self-sustenance. Unemployment, an aspect of psychosocial rehabilitation of the disabled is the best way out because getting them on job is like given them a net to fish than given them the fish that will not last long. Being on a permanent job include in them a sense of worth, belongings and relevance to the society. When one is psychologically adjusted the totality of his personality will be adjusted.

Rehabilitation Setting For the Disabled

For the disabled to be placed into any of the following rehabilitation Programme settings the following factors are determinants.

   i.   The nature and severity of the child's disabilities.
   ii.   Psychological and social need of the child,
   iii.   The strength (abilities) and weakness (inabilities in disabilities),
   iv.   Availability of Rehabilitation Programme setting.
   v.   The parent opinion, financial status, exposure and awareness of the existence of the available rehabilitation Programme /settings.

The Settings are:

   i.   Special school (Day school/ residential)
   ii.   Integral special schools are:
    -   Total integration/ inclusive education programme.
    -   Partial integration/special unit within regular school setting.
   iii.   Itinerant services provision.
   iv.   Hospitals based educational/Rehabilitation services.
   v.   Home treatment service

vi.   Resource room services for the disabled.

vii.   Vocational rehabilitation centers for the disabled.

viii.   Community based vocational Rehabilitation centers.

The Basic Steps in Rehabilitation

a. **Identification:** Rehabilitation affords kicks off with the initial suspicious by the very concerned observant parent and identification by the regular class teacher the referral agents of rehabilitation are the parents, teachers, concerned neighbors and medical practitioners. The rehabilitation process is a multi-stage effort of team of multi- disciplinary professionals and special educators.

b. **Creating Rapport**: The first step in rehabilitation is for the rehabilitation to create rapport with the rehabilitee; through friendly interaction with the rehabilitee and their guardian or sponsors and/ or their parents during the first contact session will create an atmosphere of individual opening-up to reveal all diagnosis and Programme planning.

c. **Case History:** Through such discussions detailed case history of child could be documented the case history is the historical documentation of the trend of the archeology of the condition tracing the occurrence from the period of the conception, the labor, the delivery, infancy, the childhood , till date, the information to be documented include:

-   The bio-data
-   Family History.
-   Premorbid state: This is detailed condition of the rehabilitee before the onset of the disability.
-   Medical History e.g. illness during pregnancy.
-   Developmental milestone: Age when reflexes is attained e.g.   Age of holding head upright, age of sitting with or without support, age of crawling, age of standing with or without support; age of walking and also language development etc.

d. **Differential Diagnosis:** Lerner (2000) posit three stages of Diagnosis: pre-referral, referral and assessment stage. The establishment of the real problems involves a joint effort of multi-disciplinary or professionals. Such as: Medical practitioners, psychometrics, special educations audiologist psychologist guidance and councilor, social workers, etc.

e. **Referral:** There may be need for referral to other professional such as surgeons, physiotherapist psychometric, social workers, speech therapist, and psychologist.

f. **Programme planning:** At this stage rehabilitative goals objectives hypothesis will be formulated the individualized educational programme (IEP) will be design the rehabilitative packages will be designed as well as evaluation strategy.

g. Evaluation:

h. Rehabilitation programme implementation.

i. Termination of rehabilitation:

j. Follow-up:

Goals of Rehabilitation

i. Rehabilitation is aimed at training the disabled person in order for him to acquire skills which will make him/her-self-reliance.

ii. The Rehabilitation training help the handicapped individual in their employment in their family or community.

iii. Through rehabilitation training the blind learned how to move independently and be carrying out their activities on their own.

iv. Rehabilitation help in breaching the gap created in the society by eradicating the prejudice and discrimination the disabled individual experience in the course of working or interaction their communities.

v. It enable them have a job to cater for themselves and their families.

vi.   The most important goal of rehabilitation service is to make the disable person live a useful and productive life and makes the disabled live good life.

Categories of individuals who require rehabilitation in the societies.

i.   The visual impaired (The blind).
ii.   The Hearing impaired (The deaf).
iii.   The emotionally disturbed (deviant delinquent and juvenile delinquencies).
iv.   Behavior disorder (hot tempered).
v.   The age (80-95 years old).
vi.   The youth (20-38 years old).
vii.   The physical handicapped (e.g. orthopedic child).
viii.   The epileptic child.
ix.   Prostitutes.
x.   Street baggers.
xi.   Armed Robbers.
xii.   Drug addicts.(Alcoholism).
xiii.   The unemployed.
xiv.   The destitute.

SECTION FIVE:

INDEPENDENT DAILY LIVING AND BASIC WORK SKILLS TRAINING FOR PERSON WITH SPECIAL NEEDS.

Introduction:

The goal of any form of rehabilitation is to develop the basic skills needed for cognitive, psycho-motor, psycho-social and vocational functionality of an individual; so that he/she; could perform task expected of him/her, independently of others to a certain extend. Every human being need to acquire some basic independent and basic work skills training, which are acquired directly and indirectly through exposure to some experiences. During the developmental stages of human life, such skills are systematically established in an individual. The person with special needs; no matter the type or variety of their disabilities need independent living and basic work skills training. Because of the handicapping nature of the disability and the visually impaired, the physically impaired and the mentally retarded individuals, any rehabilitation Programme, packaged for them most include independent living and basic work skills training. This chapter focuses on the: Independent living and basic work skills can be explained as; the basic daily skills required of an individual to function independently; so that he/she will be functionally intergrade to the mainstream of the inclusive setting of his/her society. The independent living and basic work skills are the survival skills, daily living skills, social skills and the adjustment skills that the individual need to acquired, for him to keep his body and soul together in harmony, these are the essential skills require for one to effectively take care of one's body, materials, surroundings (human and material) on daily basis. These skills are the basic personal hygiene, vocational pre-vocational skills require of an individual survival, keeping fit and generating income for self-maintenance.

Types of Basic Independent Daily Living Skills and Basic Work Skills Training

Edger Doll (1965) classified them as follows

- Self-help General skills
- Self-help Dressing skills
- Self-help Eating skills
- Communication skills
- Socialization skills
- Locomotion skills
- Occupation skills
- Self-Direction skills

a.   Self-Help General Skills

These are the general development of milestone skills involved in physical growth and these include

i.   Learning to hold head upright
ii.   Learning balancing the head
iii.   Learning to sit with or without support
iv.   Crawling
v.   Standing with and without support
vi.   Maintaining good pasture (that is sitting upright; walking upright without bending the spine)
vii.   Reaching for object.
viii. Overcoming simple obstacle like moving over a bench without getting hurt, walking without bumping on object, walking without sliding on solid objects.
ix.   Toileting skills include:
- Knowing that he should go to the toilet

- Reaching to the toilet and the potty.
- Controlling the bowel before reaching the toilet or potty.
- Removing the pant and wearing the pant.
- Sitting on the closet; potty without soiling self, or the dressings, or the floor or the wall.
- Cleaning up by self after toileting.

b. Self-Help Dressing Skills

These teaches the following dressing and their appropriate usages.

i. Identifying type of dressing and appropriate usage is thus identify shirt, blouse / trouser, tie, underwear, socks etc. And being able to identify and differentiate house wears from out wears (accession wear).

ii. Care for the hair. These include the identification of comb, hair cream, and hair accessories. It also include the combing the hair in acceptance direction and manner.

iii. Buttoning and unbuttoning of the short and dressings without assistance.

iv. Pulling the zip up and down,

v. Lacing and unlacing the shoes, and canvas wearing without assistance,

vi. Wearing the left shoe on the right leg and the right shoe on the left leg.

vii. Wearing shoes and removing appropriately without assistance.

viii. Wearing dress and undressing without assistance,

ix. Folding the dressing and arranging them in the boxes; wardrobe suitcases,

x. Washing underwear first, wearing dress from head and pilling it down the body without tearing them.

xi. Personal hygiene skills include:

xii. Bath, place, bathtub.

xiii.	Identifying bathing materials such as water, bucket, soap, towel, and sponge.
xiv.	Recognizing the importance of bathing in the bath place rather in the open places or spaces.
xv.	Bathing self-assisted and un-assisted systematically, that is from, head, neck, back, limb, trunk and towel drying self.
xvi.	Care of the teeth. That is identifying the tooth brush, toothpaste, chewing stick and other then brushing up down direction.
xvii.	General cleanness of the body .neatness cutting of nails short regularly wearing shippers always and so on.

c. Self-Help Eating Skills

These include:

i.	Recognition of different type of food carbohydrates, protein, fats, oil, minerals, vitamins, as well as their sources.
ii.	Identifying eatable food from un-eatable.
iii.	Identifying where the different type of food could be bought.
iv.	Recognition of eating and cooking utensils such as plates, pots, frying pan, bowls, dishes, sieve, cooking spoon, ladle, turning also cutleries (spoon fork knife). Also jug cups, mugs, napkins coasters tables mat.
v.	Recognizing the usage of the above utensils
vi.	Cooking the food the skill include measure of the food, identifying quantities of food stuffs to use. Washing cooking utensils before and after cooking making fire, cooking different meals and tidying up the kitchen.
vii.	Serving the food and drinks.
viii.	Setting the table, teaching table manner
ix.	Correct teaching habits.
x.	Self-care while eating at table-washing hand before and after meals, unsealing the dress while eating.

xi.   Drinking fluid such as clean drinkable water beverages
        fruits drinks.

d. Communication Skills

These includes:

i.   Expressing self without assistance,
ii.   Identifying direction as well as the following directions
iii.   Running errands
iv.   Listening skills
v.   Location of source of sound in space,
vi.   Reading skills work attack skills phonics approach, whole
        word approach and so on. Reading from the book,
        reading printing   from books newspaper cartoon
        stories reading braille, reading   sign post and so on.
vii.   Teaching eye-hand co-ordination
viii.   Recalling fast event and so on.
ix.   Braille writing for the blind.
x.   Teaching drawing of object science events persons and so
        on.
xi.   Teaching sign language to the hearing for paired persons.

e. Socialization Skills

These include:

i.   Establishing and maintenance of friendship,
ii.   Sharing things with others,
iii.   Playing in harmony with others,
iv.   Working corporately with others to perform a task and
        achieve a goal,
v.   Participating in social activities, recreation activities,
        competitive games and events,

vi.	Talking and accepting responsibilities for special things that are benefiting to others in the society
vii.	Complicit resolution and crises management,
viii.	Seeking attention and attending to others
ix.	Community development
x.	Dating and counter ships

f. Locomotion Skills

These include attainment of:

i.	The early age of developmental milestone such as: Movement from one places to another with or without assistance
ii.	Basic travel skills such as:-Going from room to room.
iii.	Going to public places such as market, the motor park, the amusement park the Schools the church, the bus stops, the neighborhood
iv.	Going to take transportation with assistance or without assistance.

g. Occupation Skills

An occupation is defined as job or employment or work done for a living. Work is define as that which a person does as an occupation in other to earn money to put the mind and soul together (to live healthy) to be socially accepted as a productive individual, and independent in productivity.

Factors That Determine the Choice of an Occupation

i.	Parental wish
ii.	Personal interest aptitude intelligence
iii.	Environmental influence which include, the value of the society places on specific occupation,

iv.   The society and what obtained the occupation that is appreciated in the rural environment may differ from that of the urban area,
v.   Peer influence
vi.   The influence of mass media programmes and advertisement.
vii.   Influence of role models within the environments
viii.   Educational background
ix.   Effect of career guidance.

Basic Work sk1lls To Be Developed in Person with Special Needs

They include:

i.   Searching for the job/How to search for the job
ii.   Dressing neatly in corporate wears.
iii.   Confidence and self-expression
iv.   Previous work experience
v.   Ability to express oneself explicitly; confidently and with humility.
vi.   Interpersonal relationship (good approach)
vii.   Proficiency on the job sough for.
viii.   Ability to cope with the job
ix.   Submission to authority
x.   Accountability

Management of Finances

i.   Saving
ii.   Cut your coat according to your size
iii.   budgeting

Management of Loan

Loan could be sourced from

i.   Bank
ii.   Cooperate society

iii.   Philanthropist
iv.   Microfinance establishment
v.   Family members
vi.   Mortgage institute
vii.   Non-governmental organization.

Management of Leisure Time

Leisure time refers to the time when one is free from duties or performing mandatory job of any kind. Leisure time does not refers to the period when one is free or out of job. Ideally after working, there should be leisure time. In other to relax oneself from routine work related tension and stress. It help to put spirit and mind in harmony. In other to enhance healthy body a sound mind is in sound body.

Leisure Time Or Hobbies Include:

i.   Games and sport
ii.   Cooking
iii.   Collection of artifacts   such as   stamp, precious stones archeological .
iv.   excavation.
v.   Traveling
vi.   Sewing
vii.   Tie and dying
viii.   Welfare services
ix.   Tourism
x.   Stoll
xi.   Community Development
xii.   Watching Television cinema movies
xiii.   Politics.

Family Life and Adjustment the Following Are What to Teach the Disabled

i.   The concept of family life and marriage.

ii.   Teach them maturation, puberty menstruation production and courtship.
iii.   Teach them the age they could start thinking about choosing a partner to be married to.
iv.   Teach them how to date and choose partner emphasis that priorities should be placed on love and not money. Materialism   or being forced to marry somebody that will not be compatible.
v.   Teach them the price they have to pay for them to be happy married.

Community Work

The three basic community works are:

- Community development within the locality
- Community organization: This refers to the non-governmental organization voluntary agencies, philanthropist who are committed to community development
- Community work may be in form of construction of social amenities, schools, link roads, bus stops, bridges and so on. It also include given financial sponsorship and needful moral support to the ember of the community taking active part in the politics in ones' country.

Community Life

i.   Teach them their civil right and civil obligation as citizen of a country,
ii.   Teach the concept of community development and the roles a citizen should play in the community

The Problems of Person with Special Needs in the Job.

i.   Discrimination by the colleagues because of lack of understanding of condition of disability and the residual potential hidden in disability,

ii.   Low productivity due to the physical limitation of the person with disability

iii.   Employers dissatisfaction with the performance of person disability,

iv.   Problem of adjustment to the job and coping with occupational hazards, such as accident, arthritis, health problem that are caused by being exposed to the routine of the job- long term period.

v.   Lack of flexibility to adjust to assign routine.

vi.   Lack of legislation for the right of persons with disabilities especially concerning employment,

vii.   Sexual immorality and various form of conduct disorder could be identified with some of them,

viii.   Insubordination to constituted authority person with disability could sometimes be disrespectful and disloyal,

ix.   The problem of not being accepted by their co-workers,

x.   Dissatisfaction with their payment and fringe benefits,

xi.   Inability, to budget time and finances properly to give room for savings,

xii.   Problems of colleague underestimating their capacity and potential of the person with disabilities,

xiii.   Dishonesty Recurrence out with some of them.

SECTION SIX

DIAGNOSTIC AND REMEDIAL MATHEMATICS

Concept of Diagnosis, Remediation and Mathematics

Diagnosis refers to the discovery of exactly what is wrong with someone or something by testing them closely, while Remediation Simply means way of dealing with a problem or making   an unsatisfactory situation better or you can say it is an aimed at correcting a fault in something or curing a problem with someone's health. Mathematics is the science of numbers and of shapes, including algebra, Geometry and Arithmetic

Goals and Objectives of Mathematics

Goal 1: Mathematics majors appreciate the power, beauty, and utility of mathematics.

Objectives:

a.   Use of mathematical language to model nature
b.   Describe classical mathematical results

Goal 2: Mathematics majors are well grounded in critical thinking, analysis, and problem solving.

Objectives:

a.   Collect useful information

b.   Organize information systematically   , '

c.   Apply information sensibly

d.   Make reasonable conjectures

e.   Develop reasonable approaches to problems

f.   Reach logical conclusion

Goal 3: Mathematics major can communicate mathematical ideas orally and in writing

Objectives:

a. Establish and main a clear focus
b. Create purposeful structure
c. Use an appropriate style
d. Assemble and present appropriate content
e. Use mathematical symbols and terminology

Goal 4: Mathematics majors understand both theoretical and applied mathematics

Objectives:

a. Read write and explain definitions and proofs.
b. Explain the basic ideas of calculus
c. Construct appropriate models
d. Apply standard methods of statistical analysis
e. Use basic numerical technique to solve problems

Goal 5: Mathematics major have the foundation for advance Technical degrees.

Objectives

a. Participate in mathematical discovery and research
b. Read, write and explain .definitions and proofs
c. Construct appropriate models
d. Apply standard methods and techniques to solve problems.

Types of Mathematical Problems Errors

Some scholars such as Deshler, Ellis, and Lenz all 1996 believe that many students with learning disabilities encounter major problems in learning mathematics so also Mr. Miller 1996, Mercer and millet 1992 all agrees that sometimes mathematics difficulties that emerge in elementary school continue throughout secondary school years. It is also found that all students with learning disabilities encountered difficulty with number concepts. But some students who observe reading disabilities do well in mathematics, showing strong aptitude in the quantitative thinking.

According to Vaughn and Wilson 1994, Engleman, Carnine, Steely, 1991 and Mastropert et al 1991 discover that studies of math's basals used in inclusive classes shows that they have the following deficiencies.

a.   Insufficient assurance that students have relevant prior knowledge for the lesson
b.   Too rapid a rate for introducing many of the concepts
c.   Lack of coherence in the presentation of mathematics strategies
d.   Poor communication and a lack of conclusiveness in many instructional activities
e.   Insufficient guided practice to help the students move from the initial teaching stage to the working independently.
f.   Not enough review to ensure that student will remember what they have learned

Problems

a.   **Problem in spatial relationships**, such as up-down, over-under top -bottom, high- low, near   - far, front - back, beginning -end and across.
b.   **Difficulties with numerical relationships**, it begins at an early age such as inability to count, match, sort, compare, and understand one - to - one i.e. manipulating object.
c.   **Poor sense of body image:** Children with poor number sense have an inaccurate or imprecise body image.

d.   **Visual perception** students with mathematics disabilities have difficulties with activities requiring visual motor and visual perception abilities so may be unable to count objects in a series by pointing to each of them and saying one two, three, four, five,

e.   **Language and reading problems** their language disorder may cause confusion with mathematics terms such as plus, take way, minus carrying, borrowing and place value arithmetic word problems are particularly difficult for these students.

f.   **Poor concepts of direction and time.** Most of them have a poor sense of direction and time. They become lost easily and cannot find their way to a friend's house or home from school. They sometimes forget whether it is morning or afternoon and even go home during the recess period, thinking the school day has ended.

g.   **Memory problems:** The computational facts of adding, subtracting, multiplying and dividing must become automatic if efficient learning is to take place, students with severe memory deficits sometime understand the underlying number system but are unable to recall number facts quickly.

h.   **Deficiencies in mathematics learning strategies.** Most of Mathematics disabilities in adolescents can be attributed to the student's lack of appropriate strategies for attacking and solving math problems.

i.   **Math anxiety.** This is an emotion based reaction to mathematics, causes individuals to freeze up when they confront math problems or when they confront math problems or when they take math tests (Slavin, 1991) it sometimes arise from the fear of school failure and loss of self-esteem.

Causes of Poor Performance in Mathematics

a. Lack of qualified teachers. Most of the teachers cut across other subjects like geo, history or bio and so on.
b. Negative attitude. Student's developed about the subject
c. Fear factor. Has brought about the feeling of inferiority and outright fear that most students feel when they confront the subject
d. School authorities have also contributed to the fact that student Find the subject difficult (DG of NMC) he further said some schools teach mathematics just once a week which he said was bad.
e. Some school authorities do not give enough time for the teaching of mathematic. Because of lack of teachers.
f. Mathematics is one that needs constant practice. A mathematics teacher while trying to emphasis the need for continuous studying in the subject told his class thus if you leave studying Math's for a day it will leave you for a week.
g. Charming mathematical education views e.g modern math's curriculum was introduced some forty years ago, then followed by new general math's unfortunately the modern math's approach compounded the mathematics problems of individual with mathematics learning disabilities.
h. Educational reform movement. This also contributed into poor performance of mathematics
i. Secondary students with mathematics disabilities: The secondary mathematics curriculum becomes more sophisticated and more abstract and is based on the presumption that the basic skills have been learned.

Techniques for Teaching Mathematics

Learning of mathematics supposed to be a gradual process it is not a matter of you. know it or you don't know it learning math's is a continues that gradually increase in strength .When mathematics learning progress, knowledge slowly builds from concrete to abstract, from incomplete to complete knowledge, and from unsystematic to systematic thinking, these are according to the findings of (Baroody and Gunsbury 1991).

In lines with the studies of (miller 1996) to assist students or learners progress from concrete to abstract learning. Three sequential levels of mathematics instruction are suggested. They are as follows:

a. **The concrete level.**
    At this level the child uses actual materials, such as objects in the environment, blocks, cubes, poker chips or place value sticks children can physically touch, move and manipulate
        these objects as they work out solutions to number problems.
b. **The representational level**.
    Once the pupil masters the skill on the concrete level, teaching continues to representation level. Which is semi concrete as students use pictures or tallies (marks on the paper) to represent the concrete objects as they do the mathematics problems.

c. **The abstract level.**
    At this level, students use the numbers only to solve mathematics problems without the help of representational pictures or tallies .

The Place of Games/Activities in the Teaching of Mathematics
a. **Sorting games:**
    Objects that differ in only one attribute, such as color or texture, and ask them to sort the objects into two different boxes e.g. if the objects differ by colour, students pattered paunected items in one box and blue items on another box. At a more advanced level, increase the complexity of the classification of the attributes e.g. movable objects from stationary objects. And

later use objects that have several overlapping attributes such as shape, color, and size you might present children with cut outs of triangles, circles, and squares   in   three   colors   (blue, yellow and red) and two sizes (small and; large).   Ask   the students to sort them according to shape and then according to color. Then ask them to discover a third way of sorting.

b. **Matching and sorting.**
The first step in the development of number concepts   is   the ability to focus on and recognizes a single object or   shape. Make the pupils search through a collection of assorted objects to find a particular type of object e.g. pupil might look in a box of colored beads or blocks for a red one, look in a box of buttons for the oval ones, sort a bagful of cardboard shapes to pick out the circles, or look in a container of nuts and bolts for the square pieces.

c. **Recognition   of groups of objects:**
Domino games, playing cards, concrete objects, felt boards, magnetic boards, card with colored disks, and mathematics work books all provide excellent materials for developing concepts of groups.

d. **Number stamp:**
Using a stamp pad and a stamp (the eraser on the end of a pencil will serve very well), the students can make a set of numerals with matching dots.

Motivation in Teaching of Mathematics

The most common features of mathematics instructions in Undergraduate, high schools as well as graduate schools is lack of motivation provided for abstract concepts. In most case ideas are introduced by way of another equally unmotivated abstract concept or with some practical often trivial. "Real world" application as justification for what we are going to inflict upon our students. As result most students view mathematics as a game with arbitrary rules set by us, that unconnected to anything. To find solutions to this problems of connotations the following motivations are used:

a. Use original sources with a wide variety of students: e.g. undergraduate at all levels both in courses already in the curriculum and in specially designed courses based entirely on original sources. How can we use original sources in our teaching? Certainly almost every mathematical idea is built upon a succession of preceding   ideas. And as one goes back along this chain. The motivation for a   problem   which started the journey becomes ever clearer

Why study original writing? For two reasons

a. By reading original sources students are brought as close as possible to the experience of mathematical creation, as well as see and feel the tenacity, the false starts cards triumph of its   practitioners, the   silent leaps which revolutionize fields and lead the way to the next cycle of tumult and passage.
b. When student read original sources, they are initiated into the way mathematics   is   practiced   through   research, publication   and discussion.

DIAGNOSTIC AND REMEDIAL READING

Concepts of Reading and Reading Disability

Reading Simply means getting meaning from a printed, written or signed message. Reading is more than just-seeing words clearly or pronouncing printed words correctly or even recognizing the meaning of isolated words. Reading is much more than getting literal meaning of the message itself: Mature reading implies evaluating, the ideas for truth, validity or importance.

According to Abbderin (1984) he described-that reading requires the reader to think, feel an image, and' he also" went ahead to define reading as- a vehicle for adventure, for exploration into   known and. unknown1areas of knowledge. Also, Oyetunde (2009) defined reading as the ability to obtain information from print, that is the ability to make sense of content of what is real.

Reading Disability: This simply means difficulties in reading. The poor reading leads to other types of problems such as opportunities for gainful employment usually decrease for students   with learning disabilities who are poor in reading and overall educational achievements.

A reading disability is a learning disability that involves an impairment of reading accuracy, speed, or comprehension and is significant enough to interfere with academic achievement and/or activities of daily life. Students with reading disabilities have average or above average intelligence but experience a disparity between their cognitive abilities and their ability to read. Their difficulties can be unexpected in relation to their age or the amount and quality of instruction they have received. In the Diagnostic and

Statistical Manual of Mental Disorders, Fifth Edition (DSM-5) (American Psychiatric Association. , 2013).

The diagnostic term "Specific Learning Disorder with Impairment in Reading" is used as outlined in Module 1 for individuals who experience difficulty with word reading accuracy, reading rate or fluency, or reading comprehension. (p. 67, DSM-5) Dyslexia is an alternate term used to describe specific reading difficulties that result from visual/perceptual difficulties with print that effect spelling, decoding, and word recognition. The term 'reading disabilities', used in this module, encompasses a range of difficulties that include word recognition, fluency, and reading comprehension.

However, it is important to note that a reading disability is not a cognitive disability. Students with reading disabilities have average or above average cognitive ability. Their difficulty is learning to read.

Characteristics of Students with Reading Disabilities

A student with a reading disability may experience difficulty in any combination of the following areas:

- **Difficulty mastering letter sounds and vocabulary:** Students with reading disabilities tend to have difficulty learning letter sounds, combinations of sounds, and vocabulary words.
- **Difficulty monitoring performance:** Students with reading disabilities are not usually adept at monitoring their own understanding of reading material.
- **Failure to apply strategies learned in a variety of contexts:** The strategies that support successful reading vary in subject/content areas and also vary from one assignment to the next. Reading a textbook, for example, requires different strategies and skills than reading a story. Students with reading disabilities do not adjust their strategies accordingly.

- **Difficulty in generalization:** Students with reading disabilities have difficulty transferring concepts that have been learned in one context to another context.
- **Memory problems:** Students with reading disabilities often demonstrate challenges with memory and have difficulty retaining their understanding from reading material.
- **Over-dependency:** Students with reading disabilities tend to be over-dependent on others for direction in their learning. This impacts reading assignments, which tend to be individual assignments.
- **Approaching a task:** Students with reading disabilities may have a history of limited success or repeated failure, and they may not approach a challenging learning task with a positive attitude.

Factors Responsible For Reading Problems
a. Home:-

This is the initial environment, where a child experience during first few years which influences the development of cognitive growth and becomes the foundation for later academic and social ability. Home provides both intellectual stimulation and emotional wellbeing. The critical relationship that develops between the infant and the mother or primary care giver is known as "bounding" which lays foundation for later emotional health. The development of ego, self-concept, and-self-esteem all depends on support and encouragement of caregivers within the home. Many events that occur in the home environment can profoundly disturb youths, such as in attitudes towards learning, cooperation, showing respect, and complying with rules and guidelines which are critical for success at school.

b. School:

Many special children associated deep set fears with the academic setting, which hinders them from tapping into unique skills and abilities. The school environment encompasses more than teaching and learning academic subject. In addition there must be expected set of behaviour reflective of the community values, 'Students whose home background did not prepare them for waiting their turn, staying, seated, asking permission etc may be difficult with the school environment.

c.   Peer groups:

Relation from an integral experience at-school, including school personnel such as. teachers, aide, administrators etc .many students, with learning disabilities not only experience academic difficulty but often have problems acquiring appropriate school behaviour.

d.   Social-Environment:

This is another impact of ecological system. Learning disabilities and emotionally disabled youngster often find the social arena one of deep frustration. And they may exhibit poor social perception abilities school learning is thus affected by unsatisfying social experience.

e.   Cultural:

During .the first 200 years of American education, multi cultural and multi - lingual settings were not uncommon. Most authorities recommend that the cultural heritage, of all-groups be recognize through bulletin boards that recognized holidays and major achievements of all advantages groups present with learning disabilities problems, originating from disabilities' which compounded by dimensions of student's cultural system. 'Thus, it appears than an understanding of the students cultural language background is essential for effective learning.

Instructional Strategies to Support Students with a Reading Disability

Good first teaching is essential for students with reading disabilities. What works for students with reading disabilities can work for other students too. There is no one solution, each student learns differently and the severity of learning needs can vary from mild to moderate to severe. Students with reading disabilities require extensive time and practice to learn the skills involved with reading. Efforts must be intense and prolonged with teaching and reading sessions that take place over a significant amount of time. It is crucial that students have access to a variety of reading materials that are meaningful, engaging, and at their level. When educators and/or the student support team select strategies and interventions for students with reading disabilities, they should consider two aspects of learning: the subject-area content that must be mastered and the cognitive processes required to learn. Direct instruction, or explicit teaching, is recommended to teach content. Strategy instruction is the way in which cognitive processes are strengthened. Rehearsal and practice is the way in which new information becomes learning. Research has shown that the most effective intervention for learning disabilities involves

- **Direct instruction:**
  Direct instruction is where teachers use explicit teaching techniques to teach a specific skill to their students. This type of instruction is teacher-directed, where a teacher typically stands at the front of a room and presents information.
  Teachers match their instruction to the task to enhance students' understanding of a topic. This technique depends on strict lesson plans with little room for variation. It does not include active learning activities such as discussions, workshops or case studies.

The six steps in direct instruction are:

- Introducing material, that is used to activate students' prior knowledge
- Presenting new material, where students begin to learn with step-by-step guides
- Guiding students, where teachers can correct mistakes early on and reteach material if needed
- Providing feedback, where teachers give students an indicator of their performance
- Practicing independently, where students individually apply the skills that they've gained
- Evaluating, where students are tested on what they've learned.

- **Strategy instruction**

A teaching method known as strategy instruction demonstrates to pupils how to learn the material or abilities they must master. It gives pupils specific instructions on how to process, retain, and communicate the knowledge they acquire, such as note-taking and thinking aloud.

Why use strategy instruction?

Strategy instruction is a powerful, lifelong tool that boosts students' cognitive and metacognitive abilities. It also boosts their confidence as learners. Here are some reasons why you might want to try it in your classroom.

Types of strategies

You can instruct pupils in two different categories of strategies: cognitive and metacognitive.

Students can learn, recall, and convey knowledge using cognitive methods, such as taking notes, employing mnemonics, or using a checklist. Students might utilize metacognitive methods as tools to "think about their thinking," or comprehend how they learn. These resources might range from self-evaluations to self-control methods.

Students use cognitive strategies to reach a learning outcome, such as solving an addition problem. They use metacognitive strategies to determine how to approach a learning goal, if they were successful in reaching it, and what they did to make that happen. Students typically use metacognitive strategies before or after a cognitive strategy.

	Cognitive	Metacognitive
What it is	Helps students reach a learning outcome (like solving a math problem)	Helps students to think about their thinking
Examples	Organization, like teaching students how to use an academic planner	Self-assessments, like reflecting on what they've learned
	Note-taking and study skills, like creating outlines and making drawings of the content	Self-instruction, like thinking aloud or modeling a process
	Advanced thinking, like organizing information sequentially or finding the cause and effect	Self-monitoring, like using a rubric to self-access whether they have completed all the expectations of the assignment
	SEL skills, like the active listening strategy called SLANT	

Strategies in the content areas	Reading: Determining the main idea and supporting details	Reading: Self-monitoring by asking, "Did I understand what I just read?"
	Writing: Developing and organizing an outline in response to a prompt	Writing: Self-editing using a checklist
	Math: Using tools like a fraction number line	Math: Thinking aloud while doing a math problem with a peer
	Science: Using a mnemonic to remember the order of the planets	Science: Self-reflecting on what they learned during a lab and what is still unclear

- **Rehearsal and practice**

Repetition is the key to a rehearsal method for learning new material. When a learner is given particular material to learn, such as a list, he will frequently repeat the information in an effort to recall it. He can either speak the words out or subvocalise them (say them to himself). The learner becomes more familiar with the material as a result of frequent practice. For many people, the discovery of their social security number, phone number, or the groceries they wish to buy causes them to employ a rehearsal approach.

The use of rehearsal techniques may be utilized to acquire relatively little quantities of information and is beneficial for acquiring "foundation information." Prior to understanding more complicated material, foundational knowledge must be acquired. For instance, understanding the commutative property of addition, or that a+b=b+a, is necessary to do more difficult algebraic operations.

Implementing rehearsal strategies to effectively meet the diverse learning needs of students

Identifying when a rehearsal method is ideal and when a different approach is required is one of the most crucial lessons you can give your students regarding rehearsal tactics. Verbal rehearsal of the numbers is a good method for particular information; no more complicated approach is required. For example, the phone number we need to memorize until we can write it down or call it. Long lists of information, however, might need to be memorized using a different approach for best outcomes. By assisting students in determining if rehearsal would best complete the work, we may improve their understanding of themselves as learners.

The learners may benefit from the rehearsal being coupled with a multimodal experience. For instance, when they sing the ABC song, many kids can simply "say" their letters. You might discover that certain learners respond better to practice techniques when they can associate the material being learnt with music or movement.

The order in which they learn things can also cause learners to develop attachments. For instance, I frequently have to provide the last four digits of my social security number while conducting business over the phone. I had to begin reciting my social security number at the beginning since that is the order in which I learnt it. You may offer a supportive atmosphere for your students' unique requirements if you are aware of the potential for different methods and preferences among them (some students may like to practice in silence, while others may prefer noise; other students may want the printed information close at hand).

It may take a lot of practice for the students to master the material to the point of automaticity if you are utilizing rehearsal to teach material that is part of a bigger idea or skill. You'll need to conduct periodic reviews after the first learning to make sure the pupils have retained the material. We've all remembered facts that, as soon as we stopped practicing, we swiftly forgot.

How do you choose which rehearsal technique to employ?

- Think about how your pupils want to practice knowledge, and try to offer as many different options as you can. Encourage your pupils to write songs or dances that correspond with the lessons they will be learning.
- Making a game out of the practice sessions is also beneficial. The following are some suggestions:
- When the bean bag is thrown to them, the students recite information. Then they pass it to a different pupil or return it to the teacher.
- **Choral Response:** Students give a collective response using knowledge they have practiced (particularly useful at the start of rehearsal).
- **Team competition:** Students respond individually to questions from the teacher that need memorized material in order to score points for their team.

How would you design your own rehearsal plan?

- Examine the material that has to be taught in order to decide if rehearsal is the most effective strategy. If so,
- Make a decision about how the students will practice: individually, in pairs or groups, as a class, or a combination of these.
- Group rehearsal should be included if the information is significant to the whole group and/or if it adds to a bigger idea or plan.
- Put the facts in the most logical sequence you can think of. This makes it simpler to memorize the information.
- Be willing to take it into consideration if pupils need to reorder the knowledge, but do not jeopardize their ability to learn. For

instance, it could be simpler for some students to practice the seasons out of sequence, but would they learn as much as a result?
- To ensure that the rehearsal's format—games, songs, dances, etc.—facilitates comprehension rather than causes confusion, keep in mind the student abilities.
- Information that has to be studied and paid attention to.
- Lead the class in the rehearsal process.
- Boost both the pupils' ability to employ rehearsal and their understanding of the content.

Causes of Learning Disabilities

(Kirk, S. A., Gallagher, J. J., Anastasiow, N. J., & Coleman, M. R., 2006) fingered brain dysfunction, genetics environmental deprivation malnutrition and biochemical factors.

General Effects of Reading Disorder on Learning

a. Truancy,
b. **Withdrawal.** They isolate themselves from any activities taking place.
c. **Disruptiveness:** Some children tend to find themselves in trouble with others with because of their purposeful behavior e.g. unnecessary noise in the class, jokes, jumping' out of seat, fighting, pinching laughing shouting, cracking jokes hitting- and calling names. Because of hatred for others.
d. **Task avoidance:** They give up trying when they encounter difficulty, fear falling when assignment given at the time of submitting they give excuses for not completing the assignment.
e. **Attention Deficit:.** A disorder that includes difficulty staying focused and paying attention, difficulty controlling behavior and hyperactivity. Although ADHD is not considered a learning disability, research indicates that from 30-50 percent of children with ADHD also have a specific learning disability, and that the two conditions can interact to make learning extremely

challenging. Many children with learning problems are easily distracted. Their attention may led Away from the assigned task by any noise motion, light or colour. And normally have difficulties in learning to   pay   attention   to   meaningful stimuli e.g. school lesson and attends to less meaningful e.g. noise outside the class.

f. **Achievement anxiety:** When individual fails to meet up with challenges in life, it may lead to anxiety.

g. **Low academic Achievement:** Their inability to interact with others. Affects the academic achievement of these children. Effective learning is much more successful' when you interact with others.

h. **Disorganization**: These type of children are usually disorganized. They are untidy and careless in whatever they do.

i. **Poor Self Concepts:** Most of these type of -children do not have confidence in themselves. They never believe they can contribute a meaningful learning

Identification of Learners with Reading Disabilities

The common characteristics of children with reading problem or disorders are as follows:

a. Difficulty in identifying single words
b. Problems of understanding sound in words, sound order or rhyme.
c. Problem with spelling
d. Transposing letters into words
e. Omitting or substituting words
f. Poor reading comprehension.
g. Slow reading speed (oral or silent).

In addition to these symptoms, children with reading disorder often have other delays or learning problems such as:

a. Delays 'in spoken language

b.   Confusion with direction, right/left handedness
c.   Confusion with opposite (up/down, early/late)
d.   Mathematics disorder-
e.   Disorder to written expression

Diagnoses of Reading Disorder, Assessment, Measures

Important information are sought from other school personnel's who deal with the child such as lunch aids, school nurses, principal as well as parental involvement can -be very useful.

Various Assessment techniques have been used in the classroom which are designed to serve any of the following purpose.

a.   To clearly and objectively describe the problem.
b.   To clearly established factors-influencing the problem
c.   To aid in making decision concerning treatment
d.   To evaluate the effect of treatment
e.   To provide information regarding the possible decrease or increase in the severity of the problem following treatment
f.   To collect information for teachers in teaching the child in the future.

Types of Assessment in Which Teachers Can Implement

a) Anecdotal Record:

It is a short paragraph which give a brief description of the student's behavior at one time, and provide insight into a particular behavior and a basis of 'specific teaching strategy. It also concern about what everyone else is doing and it is used to be a short paragraph notes for general evaluation of the problem e.g. Usman ignores a pleads to return to .his seat and work, but is constantly seeking for an - attention, Usman's problems includes fighting, inappropriate concern for the other children's activities.

2. Assessment Tool:

Checklists and accomplishment charts are useful tools for assisting students in learning. These resources promote participation from the students in the learning process as well as in their assessments.

Students can advance just by setting targets and criteria with you since they will have a better knowledge of what they need to accomplish to fulfill their potential.

Tools that establish precise criteria, such as checklists, rating scales, and rubrics, enable instructors and students to gather data and create opinions on what pupils know and are capable of doing in relation to the outcomes. They provide organized methods for gathering information about certain behaviors, abilities, and knowledge.

The quality of the descriptors selected for assessment has a significant impact on the information obtained through the use of checklists, grading scales, and rubrics. The students' ability to profit from the evaluation and comprehend the comments given also depends on their active participation in it.

Checklists, rating scales, and rubrics are used to:

- Before gathering and evaluating data on students' work, provide tools for systematic observation recording and self-assessment.
- Also, provide samples of criteria for students to consider. Record the development of specific skills, strategies, attitudes, and behaviors required for demonstrating learning.
- Clarify students' instructional needs by presenting a record of recent successes.

Checklists are assessment tools that provide precise criteria that may be used by teachers and students to determine skill growth or advancement. For every topic and with students in grades JK through 12, checklists are acceptable. Checklists provide a technique to systematically arrange data on a student or group of students and outline abilities, attitudes, tactics, and behaviors for evaluation (Winebenner, 2008).

In general, a checklist consists of a collection of statements that individually correspond to a set of requirements. individually statement's response can be either "Yes" or "No," or "Done" or "Not Done." Checklists may be used by an individual student, a group of students, or an entire class; they may be "single use" or intended for repeated use.

Checklists' Objectives

- To give students resources they may utilize for self-evaluation;
- To provide instruments for consistently capturing observations;
- In the start of a project or learning activity, provide students examples of the criteria they will need to meet;
- To identify students' learning requirements by summarizing prior learning, and to record the growth of the abilities, techniques, attitudes, and behaviors required for effective learning.
- Checklists can be used to inform a student's parents about their learning.

The straightforward process of making and utilizing a checklist may add a sense of order to a student's life who has learning difficulties (LDs). Giving children with LDs and ADHD methods to overcome these shortcomings is crucial since executive functions, the many cognitive processes that individuals utilize to manage their own behavior, may be a problem for them.

Creating Your Own Checklists
Teachers must: in order to build checklists

- Consider the present curriculum's learning objectives, standards, and units of study;
- Make sure descriptions and indications are precise, understandable, and easy to spot;
- Get your pupils involved in developing acceptable indicators. What, for instance, are the signs of a convincing text?

- Ensure that checklists, grading rubrics, and accomplishment charts are date-stamped to track progress over a certain time period;
- Make sure anecdotal remarks are allowed on checklists because they are frequently necessary;
- Use general models to get the students used to them and to make it simple to add criteria and indications dependent on the activity being evaluated.
- Encourage your pupils to make and utilize their own checklists so they may evaluate their own progress and establish personal learning objectives

Achievement Charts

Achievement charts are benchmarks that establish requirements for work or goods. They feature a number of indicators for each level of performance and are based on standards. They are evaluation instruments that record performance in accordance with precisely stated standards. They are created by educators and students and allow teachers to conduct in-depth evaluations (Winebenner, 2008).

Benefits of Achievement Charts

- They give more particular information regarding teaching and evaluation when compared to checklists;
- They contain specific quality indicators on which to base judgments;
- They allow students to assess their own work or receive feedback from classmates;
- They enable a detailed and thorough assessment of a student's strengths as well as areas of a skill or subject where there is room for improvement; and they clearly explain to students what is expected of them at the start of a project or task.

-      They provide students the opportunity to establish standards for producing high-quality goods and appreciating the caliber of the methods they employ.

Achievement charts should be made with as much student input as feasible. Start by defining what constitutes high-quality work. Once the "standard" has been established, it is simple to specify what constitutes acceptable and unacceptable performance.

The finest achievement charts feature three to five levels to enable a job or product to be evaluated objectively.

When these charts have been improved and compiled in a collection of examples of work demonstrating what is acceptable and what is great, they are especially helpful. The students can then take inspiration from a series of work samples.

High school students may utilize achievement charts for marking. After assigning a degree of performance to each mark, sum the scores.

Child: Benjamin Date	**Teacher: Yusuf Isah**
a) Bites nails b) Hits other children c) Talks out of torn d) Prefers to play by himself e) Fails to complete assignment f) Given order to other children (Bullying) g) Is restless h) Is jealous of attention pay to other children i) Has feeling of inferiority j) Lacks interest in Classroom Activities	

The Rating Scale

Using rating scales, teachers can describe the intensity or frequency of a learner's behaviors, abilities, and tactics. In keeping with the light switch comparison, a rating scale is comparable to a dimmer switch that offers several performance levels. In order to describe the standard or frequency of student work, rating scales list the criteria and offer three or four answer options.

Rating scales can be used by teachers to document observations and by students for self-evaluation. It helps students identify certain areas of strength and development when teachers encourage them to utilize descriptive terms like always, usually, occasionally, and never. Students can use rating scales to help them set objectives and enhance performance. In a scale of ratings, the descriptive word has greater weight than the corresponding number. The tool is more reliable the more exact and detailed the phrases are for each scale point.

Descriptors with easily understood metrics, such frequency, are used in effective rating systems. Scales that employ subjective descriptors of quality, such fair, outstanding, or exceptional, perform less well since the single adjective does not sufficiently describe the criteria that are expressed at each of these scale points.

The Rubrics

A collection of criteria is used in rubrics to assess a student's performance. They are made up of a predetermined measuring scale and a thorough explanation of the traits associated with each degree of performance. These descriptions emphasize quality over quantity, focusing instead on the number of paragraphs, the number of examples used to illustrate a point, and the amount of typographical mistakes. In order to assess student performance and include the results in a grade for reporting reasons, rubrics are frequently utilized. Rubrics can improve scoring's consistency and dependability.

A set of precise criteria are used in rubrics to assess student achievement. They may be applied to evaluate people or organizations, and like rating scales, they can be compared across time.

Creating scoring criteria and rubrics

More educators are seeing the value of using rubrics to communicate expectations to students in a clear, succinct, and direct manner. When rubrics are included in a teaching resource, there are possibilities to think about what learning demonstrations should look like and to characterize the stages of how knowledge, understandings, and abilities develop. For rubrics to be most useful, it must be possible for students to follow the level of mastery as their knowledge and abilities grow.

While feasible, students' feedback should be included while creating rubrics. Determining what great work looks like in terms of the learning objectives is a smart place to start. It's important to utilize achievements as examples to show kids what a good or respectable performance looks like. Students can use this as a library of excellent work to refer to. Once the benchmark has been set, it is simple to describe what excellent and subpar performance levels look like. The finest rubrics allow for distinctions in the evaluation of the task or product by having three to five descriptive levels. By giving each level in a rubric a score, summative purposes can utilize rubrics to measure marks.

When creating a rubric, take into account the following:

- What are the task's specific results?
- Do the pupils have any prior knowledge of this or a job similar to it?
- What constitutes a stellar performance? What characteristics set a good reaction apart from others?
- What does the rest of the performance quality spectrum look like in terms of responses?

- Is there a qualitative difference between each description and the others?
- Are there the same amounts of descriptions for each quality level?
- Do kids and others have an easy time understanding the differences?

Create criteria to define the Acceptable level first. As you proceed up the scale, use Bloom's taxonomy to uncover distinguishing factors. The evaluation criteria should not stray from the first performance challenge but rather highlight the higher order thinking abilities that students might exhibit while still adhering to the guidelines of the initial work.

Take into account the following recommendations while creating a rubric's grading criteria and quality levels.

- **The standard of excellence** level is level 4. All components of the work should be described as exceeding grade level standards and demonstrating exceptional performance or knowledge. What a "Wow!"
- Level 3 is **the degree of perfection** that is approaching. Descriptions should highlight any areas of the work that go above and beyond what is expected at the grade level and show strong performance or comprehension. A resounding "Yes!"
- **Meets accepted standard** is Level 2. The minimum competencies required to satisfy grade-level goals should be indicated at this level. Although there are some mistakes and the mastery is not complete, performance and comprehension are growing or evolving. A "On the right track, but..." is what this is.
- Level 1: **Does not yet fulfill minimum requirements**. This level denotes what falls short of the standards for the grade and shows that the learner has significant mistakes, omissions, or misunderstandings. The answer is "No, but..." To assist the

pupil progress, the instructor must decide on the best course of action.

Selecting and Designing Remedial Programmes

The professional in the field of learning disabilities believes that 3 criteria must be identified before we say that a person is learning disabled and' classification can be undertaken, (Mba, 1995) cited criteria which include.

a. A discrepancy between the person's potential and actual achievement.
b. The need to exclude the person from his peers for personalized help
c. The need for special education services for the person.

The classification of learning disabilities are sometimes' carried out according -to the degree .of learning difficulties which may include the following:

- **Mild Learning Disabilities**: This degree of learning disabilities is not serious. It is however, serious enough to attract attention of parents and teachers. If the child is not assisted the condition may become worse.
- **Moderate Learning disabilities:** The level of learning disabilities is usually referred to as "serious" and the child needs an intensive assistance in his school work. Without this assistance in terms of   materials and methods the child may not learn.
- **Severe Learning Disabilities:** The degree of learning disabilities at this level is very serious. The child at this level can not learn except when it is provided with"
    -   Special materials
    -   Special methods
    -   Individuals instruction

Assessment and Classification (Selecting Designed Remedial Programmes)

The essential purpose of assessment is classification. This is the process of identifying whether a Student has learning difficulties so as to determine the student's eligibility for special services. And Lo gather information that helps plan .instruction to improve the students learning. The plan for assessment must integrate information about the following principles.

- Skills a child mastered
- Under what condition the child is able to demonstrate skills.
- The skill child has failed to master.
- How condition of a mastered test can be alerted, so that the child demonstrate mastery.
- Observation of performance that can be used to generate principles of instruction, to enable the child to use strengths to learn functional knowledge and skills more efficiently.

When learning disabilities has evolved during the past years, various' approaches have emerged to assist in the diagnosis of children's learning difficulties. (Bateman, 2023) has discussed several approaches to the diagnosis of children's learning problems.

- **Etiological approach:** In this approach, severe learning difficulties may be seen as being due to the problem of anoxia sustained at the time of birth or hyperkinetic syndrome associated with central nervous system dysfunction. This approach is useful primarily in identifying factors associated with children's .learning difficulties so that subsequent preventive measures can be 'implemented- (Bateman, 2023) terms the diagnostic- Remedial Approach as a means of identify "How to teach" diagnostic procedure were implemented in an effort to identify strengths and weakness of the learner in terms of preferred' modalities for learning as well as pattern of perceptual and cognitive abilities.

- **Referenced Test:** Is usually an informal measures designed to identify special or specific knowledge a child has learn and knowledge that hasn't been learnt. The child's performance is not. compared with performance of a norm group. Criterion referred measures range from the simple assessment of alphabet letters a child can and can not name . to a more elaborate comprehensive assessment such as the Brigance diagnostic inventory of basic skills (Bateman, 2023). Criterion reference test are ways to measure a student mastery of specific skills. The teacher can see acceptable criterion form mastery in computational skill when that performance level is reached, the students is taught the next skill in the sequence.

Criterion-referenced tests are usually contrasted with norm referenced test. Criterion referenced test' describe rather than compare performance measuring levels rather than grade" levels in contrast, norm, referenced test, compare the pupils, performance to that of other children of the same age.

Criterion referenced test are useful they provide means of accountability while it is often difficult to show that a students has improved in term of percentiles stamina's or even grade level score, the teachers can know that the students has learned certain specific skill in term of mastery of criterion referenced measure so instruction can, be directed toward teaching- skills not yet let learned, as it deals with-observable behavior rather than inferred processes upon which academic learning is measured or assumed.

- **Diagnostic teaching:** This is an extension of the assessment of information while teaching the students. After giving test, the teachers still has much to learn about the student and can do so by developing lessons that test simultaneously and by nothing the students reactions to these lessons. Diagnostic teaching is also referred to as 'trial lesson or "teaching probes".
Any plan for diagnosis integrate information about the following principles.

- Skills a child has mastered.
- Under what conditions the child is able to demonstrate those skills
- The skills the child has failed to master
- How-conditions of un-mastered test can be altered so that the child can demonstrate mastery.
- Observation of performance that can be used to generate principles of instruction to enable the child to use strengths, to learn functional knowledge and skills more efficiently.

Development Instructional Materials for Remediation

Evaluation of language learners for potential LDS must take into account a number of factors, including native language and literacy abilities, English language and literacy abilities, cultural considerations and academic performance, family and developmental history, education, history, and the type of prior reading instruction. Whenever possible, formal assessments should include tests given in and created for the native language.

English language assessments should always be used with extreme caution because they can sometimes reveal a lack of exposure to the language or a typical pattern of growth in learning a second language, as in the case of an English language learner with suspected learning disabilities who receives a low score on an English vocabulary test. This indicates a linguistic disability rather than a lack of exposure to English. This demonstrates that the kid will gain from learning vocabulary in English.

Nonetheless, for those English language learners who struggle with the language. The following trends in reading abilities raise the risk of a learning problem.

- The child has a history of oral .language delay or disability in the native language.

-   The child has had difficulty in developing literacy skills in the native language (assuming adequate instruction in native language).
-   There is family history of reading difficulties in parents, sibling or other close relative's language assuming adequate opportunity to learn to read).
-   The child has specific language weakness, such as poor phonemic awareness, in the native language as well as in English.

References

American Psychiatric Association. . (2013). *Diagnostic and statistical manual of mental disorders: Fifth Edition. .* Arlington,: VA: American Psychiatric Association. .

Bariroh, S. (2018). The Influence of Parents' Involvement on Children with Special Needs' Motivation and Learning Achievement. *International Education Studies*, Vol. 11, No. 4; 2018.

Bateman, B. (2023). Three Approaches to Diagnosis and Educational Planning for Children with Learning Disabilities First published July 1967. *Human Institute on Dissabilities* , Volume 2, Issue 4 https://doi.org/10.1177/10534512670020040.

Pandey, D. S. (2016). *Guidance and Counseling in Education.* New Delhi : VIKAS Publishing House PVT LTD .

Parankimalil, J. (2015). *Meaning and Definition of Guidance.* https://johnparankimalil.wordpress.com/2015/01/16/meaning-and-definition-of-guidance/.

Paul Mupa, Tendeukai Isaac Chinooneka. (2015). Factors contributing to ineffective teaching and learning in. *Journal of Education and Practice*, ISSN 2222-1735 (Paper) ISSN 2222-288X (Online) Vol.6, No.19.

Winebenner, S. (2008). *D. Demers adaptation of Teaching Kids with Learning Difficulties in the Regular Classroom entitled Enseigner aux élèves en difficulté en classe régulière. .* Montreal: Les Éditions de la Chenelière.

SECTION EIGHT

DISORDERS OF WRITING

Concept and Type of Writing Disorder

A learning disability known as disorder of written expression occurs when a person's ability to communicate in writing is significantly below the level that would be anticipated based on their age, intelligence, life experiences, educational background, or physical limitations. Both the actual reproduction of letters and words and the structuring of ideas and concepts in written compositions are impacted by this handicap.

The actual writing involves number of very distinct skills, including the ability to keep one idea in mind, to formula the idea in words, to plan the correct graphic form for each letter and words, to correctly manipulate the writing instrument, and to have sufficient visual and motor memory.

The various type of skill deficiency involved in Handwriting are: Spelling and writing expression problem. There are several definition of writing disorder and these include the following:

(Peter J. Chung, Dilip R. Patel, Iman Nizami, 2019) refers to disorder of writing or problem as in the inability to put thought into a writing expression Dysgraphia. It can also refers to physical difficulty forming words and letter, it also entail the struggle to organize thoughts on paper.

The international Dyslexia association used the term "Dysgraphia" exclusively to refer to difficulties with hand writing therefore, disorder in writing may generally refers to the inability for a person to organized his thoughts and expression into writing such that can be read and understood by others.

Writing difficulties are referred to as dysgraphia. Many professionals see dysgraphia as difficulties with the transcribing skillset. We can generate writing thanks to our handwriting, typing, and spelling abilities.

Dysgraphia is a neurological disorder and learning difference in which a person has trouble writing at an appropriate level for their age as earlier stated. This can include problems with writing itself or problems with turning thoughts into written language. Dysgraphia can be controlled with programs that teach you new writing techniques.

Writing difficulties aren't technically recognized as a symptom of dysgraphia. Written expression disorder is the term for such type of learning difficulty. However, when people have trouble with transcribing, it might interfere with their ability to think through and communicate their thoughts.

Dysgraphia, for instance, might cause some people to write more slowly than others. That may have an impact on how well they write. Furthermore, because it is difficult for them to form the letters when writing, they frequently struggle with spelling.

Dysgraphia has nothing to do with IQ. The difficulties are frequently brought on by poor motor abilities. With assistance, their abilities can develop. Additionally, those who have dysgraphia may be qualified to use modifications at the office or in the classroom.

Writing

Writing is the process of expressing ideas via the use of written symbols, such as letters or the visual elements that make up words. Sentences are formed from words, and these sentences are then broken up into longer paragraphs and frequently into other discourse genres (narrative, explanatory, persuasive, lyrical, etc.).

The following are examples of writing:

Planning, organizing, drafting, reflecting on, revising, and editing written content; addressing the demands of a specific audience and communicating the text's goal (such as persuasion); The result of the writing process is the written word.

The following elements of the literary work might be mentioned:

- Word level: morphology, spelling, and word choice
- Sentence complexity, substance, and punctuation, as well as syntax
- Organizational structure, coherence, and cohesion at the textual level
- capitalization, punctuation, and other writing rules for a written piece
- Functions of communication: informing and persuading
- Organizational structure: comparative, sequential, and chronological
- effectiveness in providing the audience's information demands

Identification or Characteristics of Writing Disorder

Written language problems present in a variety of ways, depending on the language domain(s) impacted, the degree of communication disruption, the individual's age, and the stage of linguistic development.

Children who are at risk for reading difficulties in preschool and kindergarten are likely to struggle with phonological awareness and phonics (Treiman, 2018) As they strive to acquire the abilities necessary for precise and fluid word recognition, this issue can persist.

Only once a child has completed fourth grade and above in the elementary grades, when the emphasis on reading shifts from "learning to read" to "reading to learn" (Tarnopol, 1977) and when the emphasis shifts from word recognition and spelling to reading comprehension and the use of reading comprehension strategies (Leach et al., 2003), are some children identified as having reading difficulties.

Reading difficulties may become apparent for the first time in these post-primary grades with poor reading comprehension test results. Weak higher order comprehension abilities in areas like metacognitive awareness (e.g., Anderson, 1980; Wong & Wong, 1986) and the application of comprehension techniques (e.g., Hare & Pulliam, 1980; Kletzein, 1991) are likely to go hand in hand with these challenges. When word-level decoding demands increase, comprehension problems may also be the result of moderate or covert reading acquisition issues (Peter J. Chung, Dilip R. Patel, Iman Nizami, 2019)

Children with disorder in writing may be identified through the following sign and symptoms:

- Hand writing lack of neatness and consistence of writing.
- Accurately copying letter and words (Inaccurately)
- In-ability to spell words correctly
- Incoherence or disorganized writing
- Reversals in writing or reading
- Difficulty discriminating size, shapes and colour
- Poor visual motor coordination
- Difficulty copying accurately from model
- Writing too heavy
- Writing too straight
- Too much slant
- Writing too light
- Writing too irregular
- Inability to in aster pre writing skills
- Incorrect formation of letters and words

Causes of Writing Disorders

Researches on the causes of learning disabilities and writing disorders particularly suggested that more of the available evidence is conclusive on the exact cause(s) of Writing Disorder (WD) or Learning Disorder (LD). Nevertheless certain observation and points have emerged and concluded that: -

a. Writing disability and learning disabilities (LD) generally appear to   have a genetic component writing disorders (WD) tends to run in   families so some learning disabilities generally may be inherited.
b. Teratogenic causes: Eg Alcohol lead, Cocaine etc(
c. Medical causes: E.g premature birth, diabetics, meningitis, injuries before birth, or in early childhood, probably account for some later writing problems. Children born prematurely and children who had medical problems soon after birth sometimes have learning disabilities.
d. Environmental causes: E.g Malnutrition and poor parental health care.
e. Some children develop and mature at slower rate than others in the same age group as a result, they may not be able to do the expected school work. This kind of disability is called "maturational lag".

According to (Peter J. Chung, Dilip R. Patel, Iman Nizami, 2019) learning disabilities be it, writing disorder, reading, Arithmetic disorder etc, may be caused by: -

-   Brain damage
-   Biochemical imbalance
-   Environmental (e.g. quality of teaching)

(Slavin, 1995) said, there is a possibility that poor quality of instruction may result in LD or WD (teaching impaired).

Conclusively, researchers suggested that rather than determining the causes of children problems, it is more important to determine the individual unique writing problems and need so as to design instruction that has the best chance of helping him or her to meet those needs.

Handwriting styles:

Many schools start students off on handwriting using manuscript writing, which was once called cursive.

Manuscript: This is a copy of a book, piece of music, or other document that has not yet been printed. It also refers to very old books or papers that were handwritten before the invention of printing.

The optimal method for teaching writing to a kid who has writing difficulties is still up for debate. Cursive writing, on the other hand, is an archaic handwriting style in which letters were penned together (joint). Along with having trouble forming letters, some kids also struggle with manuscript letter spacing. Words copied from chalkboards are frequently spaced erratically, and some kids leave too much space between letters and words. Others align certain letters so closely together that it is impossible to read the text.

Types of Written Language Problem

a. **Handwriting Difficulties :** Handwriting issues can affect a child's capacity to spell words in writing, communicate ideas clearly in writing, and finish writing assignments on time. Orthographic coding impairments, which require translating the abstract representation of letters to the motor motions used to write words, are linked to developmental handwriting issues (McCloskey, M., & Rapp, B. , 2017). If a child or teenager has a handwriting issue that has been identified or is suspected of existing, it is crucial to provide adjustments for them during testing and throughout teaching. On a case-by-case basis, occupational therapists can be contacted to suggest suitable adjustments (such as allowing the use of a keyboard or providing a scribe).

Handwriting has often been labeled as the concrete of all the basic academic skills. Handwriting teaching may be combined with reading and writing instruction when appropriate, as it is not just a motor skill but also a written language competence. Dysgraphia according to Jordan, (1977) some   of   the writing errors are as follows:

- Too much slant: causes by writing arm to near body, thumb too stiff, point of nib too far from finger paper in wrong direction and others.
- Writing too straight: When causes by arm to far from body, finger, too near nib, index fingers along guiding pen, incorrect position of paper.
- Writing too heavy: This is caused when pressing index fingers too heavenly, using wrong type of pen, penholder too small in diameter.
- Writing too light: These are caused by pen held too obliquely or too   straight, eyelet of pen turned to side, pen holder too large in diameter.
- Writing too angular: These are caused by thumb too stiff, pen holder too tightly held, and movement too slow.
- Writing too irregular: Which are caused by movement lack freedom, movement of hand too slow, pen gripping.
- Spacing too wide: These are normally caused by pen progresses too fast to right, excessive sweeping lateral movement.

b.   Pre – writing skill

The abilities needed to learn to write are referred to as prewriting abilities. These include the sensorimotor abilities necessary for a youngster to hold and use a pencil as well as the capacity to sketch, copy, and color. The concepts in this handout were primarily created for kids ages 4 and up. These include the sensorimotor skills that contribute to a child holding and using a pencil, and the ability to draw, copy, and colour.

Many children are unable to use handwriting skills because they have not mastered a number of pre-writing skills. An understanding of body relationship such as up, down, top and buttom, is included among the pre – requisite skills for writing. The recognition and copying different sizes and shapes, correct pencil grasp, paper position and posture are other pre – writing skill.

The ability to copy single geometric shapes are another pre writing deficit.

c.   Letter formation

The formation of various letter causes difficulty for many learning disable children. It may be challenging to teach letter formation to children, that much is certain. There are several reasons why writing letters is difficult for young people. Handwriting degrades when letters are not formed correctly. When letter structure is not emphasized, handwriting issues will be seen. Problems with letter formation result in sloppy, difficult-to-read handwriting. Let's examine some typical problems with bad handwriting. We'll talk about the benefits of mastering good letter construction for legibility. The addition, omission, or reversal of certain letters seems particularly troublesome. The most commonly reversed letters include B,D,P,Q,Y and letters like U,N,M,W are also among the letters that are frequently inverted or reversed.

d.   Manuscript writing

In most schools, beginning handwriting with manuscript writing—previously known as cursive writing—is the norm. Regarding the ideal method for teaching writing to a kid with a writing handicap, there is still considerable debate. Some kids struggle with letter formation, but they also have trouble spacing the letters in written words; words copied from the chalkboard are frequently spaced erratically. Some kids place too much space between words and letters. Other locations place certain letters so closely together that it is impossible to read the text.

e. Left handedness

Today, unlike in the past, there is widespread agreement that children should be allowed to write with their strongly preferred hand, whether it be left or right. However, there are some specific issues with left handed children that need to be briefly discussed. Many left-handed people "Hook" their hand while they write in order to improve vision and prevent smearing. The true cause of this issue is the angle of the paper.

f. Spelling

The process of translating a spoken word from a phoneme to a grapheme is known as spelling, sometimes known as phonological encoding. The capacity to divide words into phonemes (units of sound that differentiate one word from another, such as /k/ as in /kp/) and map those phonemes onto graphemes (units of letters that represent sounds, such as "c" as in "cup") in the proper sequence in written form are both necessary for spelling. Words may be spelt consistently (i.e., according to established rules) or erratically (i.e., deviating from established rules). Additionally, through phonics training, kids typically acquire spelling or graphotactic principles (Treiman, 2018)

When taking into account language of origin and history, meaning and part(s) of speech, speech sound spelling patterns, and word position limitations, only around 4% of English words are irregular, and English spelling is more predictable (Moats, 2005/2006)

Word-level reading, reading comprehension, and writing composition can be affected by spelling difficulty or advancement, as well as by the underlying language knowledge areas that support it (Apel, 2009). Spelling proficiency has an impact on other aspects of literacy because of the connections between spelling and the language domains mentioned above. This connection also contributes to the explanation of why someone might be an excellent reader but yet struggle with spelling and/or writing.

The ability to spell require a number of complex an interrelated skills, Hard-shells, (Treiman, 2018)) point out that beside general intelligence, the four factors that affects the ability to spell English words are:

i. The ability to spell words that are phonetics
ii. The ability to spell words that involves roots, prefixes, suffixes and the rules and combining them.
iii. The ability to look at a word and reproduce it later and
iv. The ability to spell the demons, an analysis of spelling errors indicates the numerous problems that might be exhibited in this area,
v. Phonic ability Spelling skills involves the ability to transpose sound (phonemes) to letter (graphemes) accurately many learning disable children have great difficulty in associating sounds with symbols, they cannot translate the sounds which they hear into letters and words.

Intervention Strategies for Hand Writing Problems

Diverse writing impairments exist. Nobody who has the illness will experience all of the symptoms. Additionally, no two people will exhibit the same symptoms in precisely the same way, to the same degree, or with the same intensity. Because of this, no one method or theory—whether it be related to social behavior, psychology, or even education—can adequately explain or treat learning difficulties in all children.

Therefore, the following are some advice and techniques that have worked well with certain kids who have learning impairments (LD) and writing disorders (WD). They include:

i. Design an individual plan (IEP): This must be done carefully using a team approach, there should be a closed collaboration amongst, social class teachers, parents, psychologist, occupational therapist, speech- language therapist, regular class teachers and others as need arises.

ii. Create learning styles by initiating compatible conditions between teacher and students, strengthening by involving Musial, auditory physical movement, rhythm and emotion

iii. Capitalize on the student strength

iv. Designing the lesson based on the individual problems

v. Teach the children pre – writing skills such as writing capital letters and small letters.

vi. Make learning concrete, majority of person with writing problems, do quite well when learning a task. It is something they can get their hand on and when it is connected to something they are curious about.

vii. Provide more opportunities to practices.

viii. Teach the child how to purposefully relax before beginning school work or task. Ensure that the child is a calm alert state (Learning state) before commencing.

ix. Provide possible reinforcement of appropriate social skills both at home and school

x. Give students passages or text to recopy

xi. Provide diagrams, shapes of different sizes for the tudents to write or copy.

xii. Teach organizational skills, study skills, and learning, strategies. This is particularly helpful for people with LD.

xiii. Evaluation can provide information to help educators develop effective specially designed instruction.

xiv. Teachers may also work on language base aspect of writing, recognition of letter clusters, and root words.

xv.   Occupational therapy can help students who have motor problems.

xvi.   Diagnostic assessment and writing test can be used to determined what specific types of problems are affecting the leaner's' writing skills. Through observation, analyzing students work and connive, language and occupational educators, can make recommendations to develop individualized instruction plans.

Summary:

The purpose of intervention is to enhance spoken and written language and communication in a way that is pertinent to the student's general education curriculum and aids in their attainment of state subject requirements.

The child's functioning in areas like hearing, cognition, and speech sound production that are connected to spoken and written language is also vital to take into account. Children also bring a variety of backgrounds to the therapeutic environment. Children who utilize African American English benefit from direct education in morphosyntax and dialect-influenced inflections.

Given that dyslexia is a written language impairment, speech-language pathologists (SLPs) have a crucial and direct role in the development of literacy in children and adolescents as well as in the diagnosis, evaluation, and treatment of such disorders. Speaking and listening skills lay the groundwork for the development of reading and writing skills; SLPs have specialized knowledge of the subsystems of language as they relate to spoken and written language as well as knowledge of the metalinguistic skills necessary for reading and writing (e.g., phonological, semantic, orthographic, and morphological awareness).

At every level, spoken and written language are intertwined; children with spoken language disorders and language impairment sometimes have trouble learning to read and write; and training in either spoken language or written language can affect development in the other modality.

References

American Psychiatric Association. . (2013). *Diagnostic and statistical manual of mental disorders: Fifth Edition. .* Arlington,: VA: American Psychiatric Association. .

McCloskey, M., & Rapp, B. . (2017). *Cognitive Neuropsychology Developmental dysgraphia: An overview and framework for research. . ,* 34(3–4), 65–82. https://doi.org/10.1080/02643294.2017.1369016.

Moats, L. C. (2005/2006). *How spelling supports reading and why it is more regular and predictable than you think. .* America: American Educator, 6, 12–16, 20–22, 42–43. https://www.aft.org/sites/default/files/periodicals/Moats.pdf [PDF].

Peter J. Chung, Dilip R. Patel, Iman Nizami. (2019). Disorder of written expression and dysgraphia: definition,. *Translational Paediatrics,* Submitted Oct 22, 2019. Accepted for publication Oct 30, 2019. : http://dx.doi.org/10.21037/tp.2019.11.01.

Tarnopol, L. a. (1977). *Brain Function and Reading Disabilities. .* Baltimore: : University Park Press.

Treiman, R. (2018). *What research tells us about reading instruction. Psychological Science in the Public Interest,.* 19(1), 1–4. https://doi.org/10.1177/1529100618772272.

SECTION NINE

LANGUAGE AND SPEECH CORRECTIONS

Defective Language and Speech

Language disorders: these are significant challenges with language comprehension or language expression. Children who struggle with receptive language may find it challenging or impossible to learn the days of the week in the correct order or obey a set of instructions, such as "pick up the suckers, wash them in the sink, and then hang them up to dry." A kid who struggles with expressive language difficulties could have a vocabulary that is too little for her age, be confused about the sequence of sounds or words ("hospital," "Animal," "wide shield winder"), and use tenses and plurals inappropriately ("Them throw a ball").

The prevention and treatment of speech problems is the focus of the particular educational discipline known as logopedics. The science of logopedics was developed for both practical and theoretical reasons, expanding from the study of language and communication in relation to the development of personality to the creation of rules and techniques for language correction, the illustration of verbal difficulties, and the stimulation of verbal behaviour. The causes of speech abnormalities must be properly understood in order to make a diagnosis and choose the most effective therapeutic intervention techniques. Speech disorders can have a variety of causes that act alone or in conjunction. Children with speech difficulties are becoming more prevalent in kindergarten settings (Deacu, A., Kilyeni, S. & Barbulescu, C. , 2018).

Language problems include stuttering, difficulty pronouncing sounds, replacing certain sounds with others, and delays in language emergence and development (Vrasmas & Stanica, 1997).

Language difficulties can result from a variety of anomalies at the level of the phono-articulatory system (mouth, teeth, lips, voice cords, and airways), as well as from a lack of parental or other adult supervision and involvement in language development. Additionally, some elements of the physical world, emotional shocks, and affective barriers might cause linguistic difficulties. These are common in kids, but adults who have had ischemic accidents or strokes can also have them (Moldovan & Ciolac, 2007).

The following are articulation problems to be aware of:
1. **Dyslalia:**
   Syllable reduction, mispronunciation, or syllable reduction of a single sound or a group of sounds, which results in unintelligibility, are characteristics of dyslalia (Bussmann, 1996).
   Dyslalia can be functional, appearing between the ages of one and six years during the phonemic development stage, or mechanical in nature and caused by biological deformities.
2. **Rhinolalia:**
   This causes altered sound pronunciation, is brought on by morpho-functional abnormalities of the palate and nasal cavity. Consonants and vowels are disrupted, the communicative function of language is significantly impacted, and speaking might become incomprehensible.
3. **Dysarthria:**
   A motor speech disease known as dysarthria is characterized by weakening or paralysis of the muscles that create speech as a result of nervous system dysfunction. You can slur your speech as a result of the injury making it harder for you to control your tongue or voice box. You can improve your communication skills by receiving speech therapy. Any number of speech-motor disorders affecting articulation, phonation, or prosody

are referred to as dysarthria and can impact the central nervous system or the peripheral nervous system. Recurrent mistakes or replacements are common in dysarthria (Bussmann, 1996). It comprises phonological articulatory system organ deficiency-related pronunciation problems. Disorders of phonation and pronunciation define it. Injuries to the central and peripheral segments are what cause this condition (Musu et al., 1997). Dysarthria patients may exhibit the following diseases: somatic (respiratory abnormalities) and emotional (irritability, intellectual instability, negativism, and indolence).

When the areas of your neurological system that regulate the muscles that let you speak are damaged, dysarthria results. Your face, throat, and breathing muscles are included in this. Dysarthria can be brought on by accidents, diseases, and neuromuscular problems (diseases that impact the nerves that govern your muscles).

Typical reasons include:

- Brain Tumors
- Stroke
- Traumatic brain Injury
- Parkinson's Disease
- Dementia
- Lyme Disease
- Cerebral Palsy
- Muscular dystrophy
- Myasthenia gravis
- Multiple sclerosis
- Amyotrophic lateral Sclerosis
- Huntington's Disease
- Injury to the lips or face.
- Injury to the vocal box, tongue, neck, or head.

Dysarthria may be inherited or develop over time:

- **Developmental:** Brain injury that occurs either during foetal development or at birth causes developmental dysarthria. For instance, dysarthria can result from cerebral palsy. Dysarthria that is still developing is common in children.
- **Acquired:** Later in life, brain injury might result in acquired dysarthria. Dysarthria, for instance, can result after a stroke, brain tumour, or Parkinson's disease. Adults frequently develop dysarthria

Dysarthria patients comprehend words. They are confident in both their message and their delivery. It's only that speaking is challenging due to muscular weakness.

Forms of Dysarthria

Dysarthria might fall into one of six types. They are arranged according to the particular area of your neurological system that is impacted. Damage to your central nervous system, which consists of your brain and spinal cord, as well as the network of nerves that carries messages throughout your body (peripheral nervous system), might cause dysarthria.

a. **Flacid Dysarthria:**

Lower motor neuron injury leads to flaccid dysarthria. Your peripheral nervous system includes your lower motor neurons. You could sound breathy and nasal when you talk if you have flaccid dysarthria.

b. **Spastic Dysarthria:**

Damage to the higher neurons on one or both sides of your brain causes spastic dysarthria. The central nervous system includes the higher neurons. Your voice may come off as strained or harsh.

c. **Ataxic Dysarthria:**

Damage to the cerebellum, a region of the brain, causes ataxic dysarthria. Your cerebellum aids in the coordination of muscle motion. Vowel and consonant pronunciation may be a challenge for you, as well as putting emphasis on the appropriate portions of words when speaking.

d. Hypokinetic Dysarthria:

Damage to the basal ganglia, a region of the brain, causes hypokinetic dysarthria. Your brain has a component called the basal ganglia that aids in controlling your muscles. Speech that sounds sluggish ("hypo"), monotonous, and inflexible is a symptom of hypokinetic dysarthria.

e. Hyperkinetic Dysarthria:

Basal ganglia injury can potentially cause hyperkinetic dysarthria. It is linked to rapid-fire ("hyper") sounds and frequently erratic speech.

f. Mixed Dysarthria:

In mixed dysarthria, two or more of the other five categories are combined. The most typical form of dysarthria is this one.

Symptoms of Dysarthria

Dysarthria's primary symptom is difficulty speaking in a way that others can comprehend. You could find it challenging to move your lips, tongue, or jaw in a way that results in crystal-clear speech.

Symptoms of dysarthria include:

- Slurred or mumbled speech when speaking.
- Speaking more slowly than expected or too rapidly.
- Talking more or less loudly than anticipated.
- Sounding monotonous, robotic, strained, breathy, raspy, or harsh.
- Speaking in fragments rather than entire phrases, with many pauses.

Disorders of rhythm and fluency include the following:

1. Dysfluency:

Commonly referred to as stuttering or stammering, is a condition in which the flow of speech is disturbed due to a lack of motor coordination in the muscles used for breathing, phonation, or articulation.

According to (Bloodstein, O and Bernstein Ratner, N , 2008), dysfluent speech occurs when there is an interruption in the timing and forward flow of speech due to the repeating of sounds, syllables, or phrases, sound extension, and/or sound blockage. These are distinct from the ordinary pauses for processing ideas or production, hesitations, or gaps in fluency since they could be marked by intense strain and effort.
Secondary behaviour (facial grimaces, head/body motions), physical tension, adverse responses, avoidance of noises, phrases, or circumstances, as well as diminished overall communication, may accompany disruptions (Coleman, 2013). A typical fluency disorders, acquired/late onset stammering, cluttering, and developmental stammering in children, young adults, and adults are all considered fluency disorders.

Speech-language Therapists (SLTs) function in dysfluency

SLTs have a special responsibility for identifying and evaluating children and adults with communication-related fluency issues. Their specialised knowledge enables them to identify the exact fluency issue, its effects, and any remaining communication abilities.

Communication problems frequently limit access to education and negatively affect many aspects of quality of life, such as employment, peer relationships, and social integration. Speech and language therapists evaluate how the condition affects the person.

2. **Autism:**
This is a serious social behaviour disease that is characterised by significant routines, stereotypical behaviours, and aberrant

responses to sensory inputs. This condition is thought to have a number of origins and manifests itself before the thirty-first month of life in early childhood (Bussmann, 1996).

Developmental impairment known as autism spectrum disorder (ASD) is brought on by variations in the brain. Some ASD sufferers have a recognised distinction, such a genetic disorder. Other factors are still unknown. ASD is thought to have a number of underlying reasons that interact to alter how people typically grow. There is still a lot we don't know about these factors and how they affect persons with ASD.

People with ASD may behave, interact, communicate, and learn differently than most other people. Frequently, their appearance does not distinguish them from others. People with ASD might have a wide range of talents. For instance, although some ASD sufferers are nonverbal, others may have superior conversational abilities. Some persons with ASD require a lot of assistance in their everyday life, while others may function independently and work.

ASD usually manifests before the age of three and can last the rest of a person's life, however symptoms occasionally become better with age. ASD symptoms might appear in some kids within the first year of life. Others might not experience symptoms until they are 24 months old or older. Some ASD children learn new skills and reach developmental milestones up to the age of 18 to 24 months, at which point they cease doing so or lose the abilities they previously possessed.

Adolescents and young adults with ASD may struggle to make and keep friends, communicate with peers and adults, or comprehend what is appropriate behaviour in the workplace or at school. They could be noticed by medical professionals if they also have disorders like anxiety, depression, or attention-deficit/hyperactivity disorder, which affect persons with ASD more frequently than those without ASD.

Symptoms and Signs

People with ASD may struggle with confined or repetitive behaviours or interests, as well as social communication and engagement. Additionally, people with ASD may learn, move, or pay attention in various ways. These qualities may make life very difficult. It is significant to remember that some individuals without ASD may also have some of these symptoms.

Diagnosis

Since there is no medical test, such as a blood test, to diagnose ASD, doing so might be challenging. To determine a diagnosis, doctors consider the child's behaviour and developmental stage. ASD can occasionally be identified in children as early as 18 months. A valid diagnosis made by a qualified expert can be assumed by the age of two.1 However, a lot of kids don't get a definitive diagnosis until they're considerably older. Some patients don't receive a diagnosis until they are teenagers or adults. People with ASD may not receive the early assistance they require as a result of this delay (Hyman, S.L., Levy, S.E., Myers, S.M., & AAP , 2020).

Treatment

The goal of current ASD therapy is to lessen symptoms that affect everyday living and quality of life. Because ASD has a distinct impact on each individual, each person with ASD has various strengths, problems, and treatment requirements. Plans for treatment typically involve a number of specialists and are tailored to the person.

The following vocal problems should be mentioned:
1. **Dysphonia:**
    Disorders of the voice are referred to medically as dysphonia
    (diss-PHONE-nee-yah). The term "dysphonia" refers to a
    variety of vocal abnormalities brought on by poor phonatory
    skills, laryngeal growths or infections, or psychological causes
    like stress or depression (Bussmann, 1996). According to
    Popescu-Neveanu (1978), pronunciation problems resulting
    from structural flaws or phonemic equipment wear can cause a
    nasal or hoarse sound.

    Poor voice quality without any visible anatomical, neurological,
    or other biological issues affecting the larynx or voice box is
    known as functional dysphonia. Additionally known as
    functional voice difficulty.

    You can have dysphonia, also known as hoarseness, if your
    voice sounds rough or harsh. Perhaps you spoke too loudly at a
    noisy restaurant, or perhaps this symptom is the result of an
    underlying medical issue. Hoarseness should go away quickly,
    but if it persists for three weeks or longer, you should consult a
    doctor.

    Hoarseness, sometimes referred to as dysphonia, is a vocal
    handicap that makes a person's voice unintentionally seem
    raspy or strained, lower in loudness or pitch. It frequently goes
    hand in hand with issues with the vocal cords located in the
    larynx (voice box). Chronic aphonia, or the inability to create
    vocal sounds, can occur in both children and adults. This
    condition requires medical treatment in order to determine what
    is causing it.

    When your voice sounds raspy, strained, or breathy, you have
    hoarseness (dysphonia). Both the pitch (how high or low your
    voice sounds) and the loudness (how loud or quiet you talk)

may vary. There are several reasons why someone could get hoarse, but luckily, most of them are not dangerous and quickly go away.

Rest is typically suggested when dysphonia first appears, but if it persists for longer than two weeks, a doctor should be seen to rule out the presence of any significant injuries and to stop dysphonia from turning into chronic aphonia, which results in a complete loss of voice. Rest, anti-inflammatories, or, depending on the circumstance, speech therapy will be needed when dysphonia has occurred, whether it was brought on by overusing the voice or by viruses and illnesses.

Types of Dysphonia

Two varieties of dysphonia exist:
- **Acute dysphonia:** Resolves with rest and symptomatic therapy and is typically self-limited.
- **Chronic dysphonia:** More complicated since it can have a variety of reasons, including congenital defects and cancer lesions.

Symptoms of Dysphonia

Hoarseness, monotonous speech, tremor in the voice, aphonia, variations in voice intensity, and loss of treble (the highest pitch) are the most typical symptoms.

In addition, there may be non-vocal symptoms including a cough, an itchy throat, and mild to moderate throat discomfort.

Causes of Dysphonia

Children's dysphonia can be brought on by neurological conditions, laryngeal abnormalities, viral infections, or

overusing the voice. The latter is the most typical reason for
adult dysphonia.

Other things including gastric reflux, smoking, infectious
conditions like laryngitis or TB, neurological laryngeal
problems, or tumours can cause dysphonia.

Diagnosis

Dysphonia cannot be diagnosed with a specialised test; instead,
it is often determined by the patient's account of their symptoms
and the quality of their voice.

An otolaryngologist may use a flexible fibre optic laryngoscope
that is put via the nose to see the vocal folds while the patient is
speaking.

Treatment

Dysphonia can be addressed by giving the voice a break and
altering lifestyle choices like quitting smoking and increasing
fluid intake. Anti-inflammatory drugs should be taken if an
infection is the source of the dysphonia.

2. **Aphonia:**

    Aphonia is a speech disease in which you can still talk, but your
    sounds are just barely or not at all audible to others. People who
    get this illness try to converse but can't be heard by others
    because it often comes on abruptly. Aphonia is categorized as a
    functional speech problem, indicating that it has more of a
    mental or neurological (brain) origin than a physical one.

    Aphonia, often known as voice loss, is the inability to speak
    beyond a whisper or to use your voice loudly enough to be
    heard. You may at times be completely speechless. On other
    occasions, you might not want to talk because you believe your

voice is unusual or odd. Exercises in voice therapy are used by medical professionals to address aphonia.

According to Bussmann (1996), aphonia is an impairment of phonation brought on by either psychogenic or organic factors, such as an illness or trauma. The paralysis of the vocal cord muscles causes the most severe voice problem, which is characterised as the inability of phonation and the entire or partial loss of voice (Popescu-Neveanu, 1978).

Types of Aphonia
Functional aphonia and psychogenic aphonia are two different types of aphonia, yet they both are believed to have the same underlying origins.

a. **Functional Aphonia:** When a person has difficulty using their larynx (voice box) and diaphragm (the muscle responsible for breathing) to create speech without obvious physical or neurological issues, this condition is known as functional aphonia.

b. **Psychogenic Aphonia:** When a person loses their voice in reaction to a traumatic or psychologically stressful incident, this condition is known as psychogenic aphonia.

Causes of Aphonia
Upper respiratory tract infections or recurring laryngitis have been linked to certain cases of aphonia, but they may not be the primary cause. A stressful or painful life experience is typically what starts aphonia.

Since it only affects 0.4% of persons between the ages of 14 and 35, this disorder is regarded as uncommon. According to studies, persons who are born with a gender preference are around 8 times more likely to develop aphonia than people who are born with a gender preference (Pachaiappan C, Sangeetha G, Balasubramanian S, Ramya Sri C., May 2020;).

Aphonia has been linked to a number of potential reasons, including:
- Anxiety,
- Fear, and depression.
- Issues with interpersonal connections

Diagnosis

As the initial stage in diagnosing aphonia, a healthcare professional will do a physical examination and go through your personal and family medical history. They must rule out any structural issues or illnesses that can make you lose your voice.

Aphonia is famously challenging to diagnose, primarily because it is frequently unrelated to any medical issue, such as vocal cord dysfunction. Aphonia is categorised as a conversion disease since it lacks a clear biological, physiologic, or neurological origin. According to one research, it can take nine to 32 weeks to get a correct diagnosis of aphonia, and multiple false positives are often made before that.

Other signs and symptoms of conversion diseases, such as aphonia, include: blindness, paralysis, non-epileptic seizures, hallucinations, motor tics, and difficulty swallowing.

In its Diagnostic and Statistical Manual of Mental Disorders (DSM-5) fifth edition, the American Psychiatric Association has included precise diagnostic criteria for identifying conversion disorders (Al-Balas HI, Abuhalaweh M, Melhem HB, Al-Balas H. , June 2021;).
- At least one symptom involves a change in motor or sensory function.

- The symptom is severe enough to cause functional impairment or considerable discomfort;
- There is no connection between the symptoms and other neurological or medical disorders;
- The symptoms are not being caused by another medical condition or mental disease.

Treatment

The most common method for treating aphonia is a mix of psychotherapy and speech therapy. A medical professional will pay close attention to any underlying conditions, stresses, or incidents that may have contributed to the disease and will consider how best to treat each one on an individual basis.

Prognosis for Aphonia

Although aphonia might be difficult to identify, it is typically treatable. Once the issue has been diagnosed, speech therapy and psychotherapy are highly successful in assisting aphoniacs in overcoming their condition (Al-Balas HI, Abuhalaweh M, Melhem HB, Al-Balas H. , June 2021;).

Therapy can totally cure most patients with aphonia. In one research, every patient who just had speech therapy made a full recovery. Aphonic individuals might restore vocal function on the first day of therapy, according to a different research.

However, a preoccupation on aphonia may result from a delayed or missing diagnosis, making the illness more challenging to cure.

The following are examples of poliform language disorders:

1. **Alalia**

    Speech delay, also known as alalia, is a disorder where a kid has trouble producing sounds or speech utilizing their lungs, vocal chords, mouth, tongue, or teeth. Due to this problem, the youngster learns words slowly and is unable to mold his or her mouth and tongue to speak normally.

A speech delay, as described by specialists, is a condition in which a youngster does not make the usual attempts to verbally communicate. This might be caused by a variety of circumstances, which is why it's crucial to include a speech-language pathologist.

There are numerous possible causes for a youngster to exhibit aralia and not be communicating in an age-appropriate manner. These may include things like the youngster being a "late bloomer" (taking a little longer than typical to talk) or having brain damage. An SLP's job is to do a process of elimination, weighing each potential reason for a speech delay, until a cause is identified.

The first step in helping a kid like Alalia who has a speech delay is to make a distinction between the speech and language aspects of the child's development.

The tongue, mouth, and vocal chords, as well as the muscles and nerves that link them to the brain, are all important in speaking. Two conditions that impair the nerve connections and speech organs are apraxia of speech and dysarthria. Cleft palates and hearing loss are two further instances in this group.

Language is the other important area that SLPs will assess. This is more brain-related and may be impacted by brain illnesses like autism or injury to the brain. The SLP will do examinations for all developmental abnormalities, as well as the several forms of brain injury that each present in a unique way.

Ability Innovations can assist in identifying the cause(s) of the speech delay, after which our speech therapists may begin treating and supervising the kid. Early intervention and evaluation by an SLP can make a significant impact for many speech-language problems that result in a speech delay.

The signs and traits of speech delay
The typical way to detect speech delay in children is to observe their language development milestones.
A kid is most likely experiencing a speech delay if she is not speaking 3-5 words by the age of one or if her vocabulary has not grown to at least 15-20 words by the age of fifteen months. When a youngster is 15 months old and still not speaking words like "ma" and "no," intervention and treatment are needed.
Speech therapy should be sought if, between the ages of 2 and 4, a kid cannot utilize words in phrases or sentences, he cannot employ consonant sounds, or he has trouble following instructions.
Oral-motor dysfunction brought on by illnesses such apraxia is another sign of speech delay.

Causes of Alalia (Speech Delay)
Physical abnormalities in the mouth, such as a malformed frenulum, lips, or palate, as well as oral-motor dysfunction, which is a deficiency or delay in the region of the brain where speech is created and sent to the mouth and tongue, are some causes that may cause speech delay in a child. Others includes:
- Delivery complications
- Hearing loss
- Viral and infectious infections
- Brain traumas in the post-natal period (after delivery)
- Prenatal traumas
- Perinatal traumas (just before or after birth)

Therapy for Speech Delay

For a kid who exhibits delayed speech, an auditory screening (hearing test) is a crucial first step, and early intervention with speech therapy is the recommended course of action. If hearing loss is an issue, the youngster may benefit from hearing aids, sign language instruction, or ear tube insertion surgery.

Speech therapy is frequently used as treatment if there is no hearing loss. If a child's weak muscle tone prevents speech, physical or occupational treatment may be necessary.

Working with a private speech pathologist or in a classroom environment are both possible in speech therapy. Speech therapists advise parents to work with their kids at home by reading aloud to them, speaking to them in a clear and concise manner, and engaging in word games like pointing out animals when out on a walk.

Speech Buddies should not be used to deal with speech delay concerns directly. However, if a kid has articulation issues, they may be able to aid them if they have experienced a speech delay.

Other Therapies effective for Speech delay includes:

Use Flashcards or Labels
An excellent technique to assist your youngster with recognizing items and speaking out these phrases is to name objects around your home with flashcards. Your child's communication skills will improve the more you speak to him or her and have him or her repeat new words.

Activate learning while playtime.
When children play, they are open to learning about both spoken and nonverbal relationships. Your youngster will learn

and say fresh words and phrases if you verbalize play activities like "catch the ball" or "give me the plane."

Short and uncomplicated is best.
Make sure the words you use to talk to your child are audible, brief, and basic. This will make it easier for your child to relate to you, which will affect how your child learns to mimic your voice and language.

Use commonplace scenarios.
Talk to your youngster as much as you can about the things he or she encounters every day. Speak out the names of the products you buy, the foods you cook, the items in your home as you go about your daily cleaning routine, and so on.

Read aloud to your kids.
Use books, ideally the ones that let you point to and identify pictures for your youngster to grasp.
The methods mentioned above may assist your child deal with the speech delay (Alalia) issue more effectively to some extent. To offer your kid the best opportunity of overcoming this speech issue, it is advised that you schedule a visit with a qualified speech therapist.

2. **Aphasia**

   A communication condition called aphasia affects how you speak. It may affect the way you write, speak, and comprehend both spoken and written language.

   Typically occurring unexpectedly after a stroke or a brain injury, aphasia. But it can also develop gradually as a result of a brain tumor that grows slowly or a degenerative condition that damages the body over time. The source and amount of the brain injury are two factors that affect how severe an aphasia is.

Aphasia is mostly treated through speech and language therapy in addition to addressing the underlying issue that causes it. The aphasic individual trains and relearns language skills as well as picking up new communication techniques. Family members frequently take part in the process, aiding the individual in communication.

You are not less intelligent or have issues with your ability to think because of aphasia. However, it can impair your capacity for straightforward communication. You can find it challenging to comprehend, read, or write if you have aphasia.

Different people are affected by aphasia in different ways, and no two persons will alter or recover in the same manner. The cause, the degree of brain injury, the support of the family, and the therapy all have a role in the severity and course of aphasia.

Aphasia comes in a variety of forms. These are often identified depending on the amount of the damage and the region of the language-dominant side of the brain that is damaged. For instance, those who have Wernicke aphasia have damage to the side of the language-dominant section of the brain whereas those who have Broca aphasia have damage to the front half of the same area of the brain.
A significant section of the language-dominant side of the brain has been damaged, leading to global aphasia.

Types of Aphasia

The Broca's Aphasia:
The French physician who made the discovery that this region of the brain governs the muscles you use to talk gave it the

moniker "Broca's area." It is a portion of your frontal lobe and is often on your left side, slightly above your temple.

It is sometimes referred to as "expressive aphasia" or "non-fluent aphasia," and it is one of the most prevalent types of the disorder. Broca's aphasia often affects the following people:

- **Fluency loss.** Broca's aphasia patients have trouble forming words. While they struggle or are unable to repeat back what you say to them, they may repeatedly speak the same words or short sentences. The most severe cases result in mutism or the ability to only create one sound at a time.

- **There is no impact on understanding.** Broca's aphasia patients are unable to talk, yet they are still able to understand what other people are saying. Additionally, they are able to detect any issues with their speech.

- **Strive to avoid repetition.** Since repetition is hampered by Broca's aphasia, a person may find it challenging to repeat back words or phrases you speak to them.

- **Other Symptoms:** Damage to Broca's area usually affects a nearby section of the brain that controls how the muscles move, especially after strokes. Because of this, people with Broca's aphasia are more likely to have some kind of paralysis on one side of their body.

Wernicke's Aphasia:

This region of the brain is named after the German neurologist who found that it regulates your capacity for comprehension and word choice when you speak. It is a portion of your temporal lobe and is often located on your left side, slightly above your ear.

Together, the Broca's and Wernicke's parts of the brain enable you to talk. Wernicke's area analyzes the words you comprehend and decides the ones to employ before sending signals to Broca's region. The impulses are sent to the muscles you use to talk once the Broca's region has determined the words to employ.

This type of aphasia is often referred to as "fluent aphasia" or "receptive aphasia," and it is also rather typical. Wernicke's aphasia often affects the following people:

- **Talking clearly.** This indicates that they have no difficulties physically speaking. However, they frequently say things that are contradictory or illogical. Those who have it could make new terms or use inappropriate language. This is referred to by experts as "word salad."
- **Issues with comprehension.** People who have this find it difficult to comprehend what others are saying. They can be able to comprehend extremely straightforward statements, but the more intricate the language or phrase, the more difficult it is to comprehend.

- **Fight against repetition.** A person with Wernicke's aphasia may find it difficult to repeat back words or phrases you speak to them since it hampers repetition.

- **Other symptoms.** Wernicke's area of the brain is close to regions of the brain that affect vision, thus individuals with this type of aphasia frequently also experience difficulties with their vision. Anosognosia (an-oh-sog-no-zh-uh), a condition where your brain can't detect or comprehend signals of a medical problem you have, is a condition that Wernicke's aphasia patients frequently experience. Therefore, individuals with this type of aphasia frequently are unaware of or unable to comprehend that they have it.

The Global Aphasia

The most severe kind of aphasia is this one. People who suffer global aphasia have trouble understanding or communicating in words. These elements are typically present.

- **Fluency loss.** People who have global aphasia find it difficult to talk out loud. The most extreme types of this might cause mutism, when a person makes no sounds at all or just little, isolated noises. Additionally, they can keep repeating single words or short sentences. This hinders their fluency since they won't be able to repeat back what you say to them.

- **Issues with comprehension.** People who have this find it difficult to comprehend what others are saying. They can be able to comprehend extremely straightforward statements, but the more intricate the language or phrase, the more difficult it is to comprehend.

- **Fight against repetition.** A person with global aphasia may find it difficult to repeat back words or phrases you speak to them.

- **Additional symptoms**: Conditions that result in significant brain damage, such as massive strokes or head traumas, can produce this type of aphasia. The injury frequently involves numerous areas of the brain and is severe, leading to other major symptoms as blindness and one-sided paralysis.

Other Forms of Aphasia
Transcortical Motor Aphasia

Although often not as severe, transcortical motor aphasia is analogous to Broca's aphasia. One significant distinction is that those who have this don't have any trouble repeating back words or sentences that you say to them.

Transcortical Sensory Aphasia

Wernicke's aphasia is comparable to this variety, albeit typically not to the same degree. Similar to the transcortical motor aphasia described above, those affected have no trouble repeating what you say. With degenerative brain disorders like Alzheimer's disease, this kind of aphasia is typical.

Conduction Aphasia

Fluency is affected but not understanding in this kind of aphasia. Those with this difficulty pronouncing words find it difficult to repeat what you say to them.

Mixed Transcortical Aphasia

he only difference between this aphasia and global aphasia is that those who have it can still repeat what others say to them.

Anomic Aphasia

This type of aphasia makes it difficult for sufferers to locate words, particularly those that describe activities or things. They frequently employ many words to convey their meaning or general terms like "thing" to get around this issue.

Other Conditions that Involves or look like Aphasia

Progressive Primary Aphasia

Despite having the word "aphasia" in the name, this condition affects the degenerative brain. People who have this syndrome eventually lose their capacity to communicate verbally, in writing, through reading, orally. This is distinct from aphasia brought on by an accident or stroke, which doesn't worsen over time. PPA can manifest in many ways with conditions including frontotemporal dementia and Alzheimer's disease.

Agraphia (the inability to write) and alexia (word blindness).

Your ability to read and write might be hampered by damage to the areas of your brain that govern speech. Although those who have alexia may see words, they cannot comprehend or read them.

Agraphia causes people to be unable to write. Although both can coexist, alexia without agraphia is an uncommon condition in which a person can write words but is unable to read what they have written.

Auditory verbal agnosia

This is a condition where a person can hear other people speaking but is unable to distinguish it from their own speech. It occurs when there is an interruption in the processing of sound or spoken words in the brain.

Signs and Symptoms of Aphasia

Aphasia is a sign of another illness, such as a brain tumor or a stroke. An aphasic individual might:
- Use terse or incomplete phrases while speaking
- Use illogical sentence structure when speaking.
- Replace one word or sound with another
- Speak incomprehensible phrases
- Having trouble finding words
- Not being able to follow conversations of others

- Not comprehend what they read Write illogical phrases

Causes of Aphasia

Any illness that harms the brain can cause aphasia. Additionally, issues that interfere with your brain's operations might cause it. These are some of the potential causes:

- Alzheimer's condition
- The aneurysms.
- Neurosurgery.
- Tumors of the brain, including cancer.
- Cerebral hypoxia, or oxygen deprivation-induced brain injury.
- Traumatic brain damage and concussion.
- Frontotemporal dementia and dementia.
- Congenital issues (conditions you are born with due of a flaw in fetal development) and developmental abnormalities.
- Epilepsy or seizures, particularly if they result in long-term brain damage.
- Genetic diseases (disorders you have at birth that you inherited from one or both parents, such Wilson's disease).
- Brain inflammation (encephalitis) brought on by bacterial, viral, or autoimmune diseases.
- Migraines (this impact is fleeting).
- Chemotherapy or radiation treatment.
- Poisons and toxins (such as heavy metal or carbon monoxide poisoning).
- Transient ischemic attacks (TIAs) or strokes.

Tests and Diagnosis

A physical examination, questioning about your past, diagnostic imaging and testing, and other procedures are used to diagnose aphasia. In certain instances, a medical professional will advise doing a number of tests to rule out other illnesses or reasons that could have consequences resembling those caused by aphasia. Here are a few instances:

- **Tests of nerve and sensory function.** These tests will confirm that a condition that resembles aphasia is not being caused by hearing issues or nerve damage.
- **Exams of the mind and memory.** These exams make sure the person's memory or cognitive skills aren't the issue.
- **Imaging and diagnostic procedures**. These exams search for lesions or indications of brain injury in the pertinent area.

What examinations will be performed to identify this condition?

When doctors suspect aphasia, they may do a number of tests. A speech-language pathologist may typically assist in identifying the kind of aphasia a person has, if any. The results of the tests may also be used to diagnose the underlying cause of the aphasia, as well as to decide if it is curable and the most effective course of therapy.

Possible tests could include:

- Blood testing (used to check for toxins and poisons, particularly specific metals like copper and immune system issues).
- CT scan (computerized tomography)
- EEG, or electroencephalogram.
- The electromyogram.
- Test of evoked potentials.
- Genetic analysis.
- MRI, or magnetic resonance imaging.
- A PET scan, or positron emission tomography.
- A lumbar puncture (spinal tap).
- X-rays

Management and Treatment
Aphasia, sadly, has no specific treatment. It is typically treated in some way, though. Treating the underlying illness is frequently the first step in treating aphasia. Quickly restoring blood flow to the afflicted part of the brain can occasionally lessen or avoid lasting damage in diseases like stroke.

Aphasia is frequently transient when it results from a temporary issue, such as a concussion, migraine, seizure, or some sort of illness. In most cases, when you recover and your brain heals as a result of therapy and time, the aphasia becomes better or disappears totally.

Speech therapy occasionally helps a person's language ability if they have sustained serious brain injury that is either long-term or permanent. These therapeutic methods can also aid a patient in developing better interpersonal skills and compensatory strategies for their aphasia. Caregivers and loved ones can participate in speech therapy so they can interact with you and assist you in the best way possible.

Assessment of Language and Speech

Speech-language evaluation is a difficult task. Integration of a range of data acquired throughout the evaluation process is necessary for rating, characterizing, and understanding a person's communication competence.

Speech, language, and communication are all related to how a person understands and communicates with others. Exams of speech, language, and communication look at both receptive and expressive language.

An evaluation of expressive language looks at how a person communicates, which might include words, gestures, and facial expressions. Receptive language testing will examine a person's ability to comprehend and interpret the words, gestures, and facial expressions of others.

According to ASHA's (2004) Preferred Practice Patterns for the Professions of Speech-Language Pathology, a thorough evaluation of speech-language pathology comprises the following elements:

- Case history, comprising information from teachers and other service providers, medical status, educational background, social background, cultural background, and language background

- Interview of the patient, client, student, and family
- Review of the cognitive, motor, visual, and auditory systems
- Observations and analysis of work samples, as well as standardized and/or non-standardized measurements of certain components of speech, spoken and non-spoken language, cognitive-communication, and swallowing function
- Determining the likelihood of successful intervention techniques and compensations
- Assessment of speech, language, cognitive-communication, and/or swallowing using standardized measures while taking verified ecological validity and cultural sensitivity into account
- Follow-up services to keep an eye on communication and swallowing status and make sure that people with recognized speech, language, cognitive-communication, and/or swallowing issues receive the right support and assistance

Sections 300.301–300.305 of the Individuals with Disabilities Education Act (IDEA, 2004)contain particular provisions relating to student evaluations in educational settings. SLPs must also adhere to local and state regulations for student evaluations.

The differences between the phrases evaluation and assessment as per IDEA Part C Guidelines should be taken into consideration. The phrase "evaluation" refers to the "procedures used by qualified personnel to determine a child's initial and continuing eligibility..." IDEA (2004), Part B mandates that an examination be thorough and examine every potential area of impairment. In order to address educational and/or behavioral problems for kids who are not reaching grade-level expectations, it is crucial for the clinician to include other assessment personnel as a part of the multidisciplinary review team (IDEA, 2004, Section 34 CFR 300.304).

When a child is eligible for early intervention services, assessment refers to "the ongoing procedures used by qualified personnel to identify the child's unique strengths and needs and the early intervention services appropriate to meet those needs...and includes the assessment of the child...and the assessment of the child's family." Part C of the IDEA, Section 303.321

Speech and Language Communication Needs
An individual's demands relate to areas of difficulty within speech, language and communication. Speech, language, and communication needs might include all of a person's understanding and communication methods or just one specific one. We identify the strengths and challenges of each child and adolescent with speech, language, and communication problems throughout an examination.

Among the demands in speech, language, and communication are:

- Paying attention and hearing
- Understanding
- Expressive words
- Receptive language Production of speech sounds
- social interaction
- Memory

Early intervention is made easier when speech, language, and communication deficits are typically detected in children. Skilled team of psychologists can assist with kids and teenagers between the ages of 0 and 25 who have speech, language, and communication problems.

For whom is a speech, language, and communication evaluation appropriate?

For people ages 0 to 25, speech, language, and communication examinations are appropriate. A worldwide evaluation of speech, language, and communication abilities is often beneficial for people who are developing their speech, language, and communication skills more slowly than their peers. A speech, language, and communication examination may be advantageous for a child or young person for a variety of reasons, including those who:

- Possess delayed or erratic speaking sounds
- Have trouble comprehending speech
- Possess trouble adhering to directions
- Have communication issues
- Demonstrate inadequate or nonexistent social skills
- Possess a lack of social skills
- Battle with the rigors of the classroom
- Having trouble maintaining eye contact
- Difficulty with gestures

An evaluation of a person's speech, language, and communication skills is a useful tool for determining their learning requirements. In order to help the child or young person with their learning and language, an evaluation may result in more research, treatments, or suggestions.

Evaluations of speech, language, and communication can be performed by educational psychologists, child psychologists, and speech-language pathologists. In order to enhance communication, speech and language therapists evaluate speech, language, and communication. Speech, language, and communication skills are evaluated by educational and child psychologists, and the results are used to help the child's or young person's learning.

Assessment Tools for Speech and Language Communication
Depending on the person, their circumstances, and the language or communication feature being evaluated, several speech, language, and communication tests may be used. Using a range of speech, language, and communication examinations, our expert team of psychologists can:

- PhAB2 - Phonological assessment battery
- Renfrew - Renfrew action picture test

- CELF 4 - Clinical evaluation of language fundamentals
- CELF- Preschool 2 - Clinical evaluation of language fundamentals – preschool
- BPVS - British picture vocabulary scale
- CCC-2 - Children's communication checklist
- AQ test - Autism quotient test
- TALC - Test of abstract language comprehension
- ACE - Assessment of comprehension and expression
- ADI-R - Autism diagnostic interview – revised
- TASIT - The awareness of social inference test
- SSIS - Social skills improvement system
- PLS - Preschool language scales
- NRDLS - New reynell developmental language scales
- YARC - York assessment of reading for comprehension
- TROG-2 - Test for reception of grammar
- TALC - Test of abstract language comprehension

List of Tools and Equipment's for Language Assessments
There are several different types of kids that are classified as deaf and hard of hearing (DHH). Their hearing thresholds, ages at which they came of age, medical and educational backgrounds, language heritages, and cultural identities are all different (IDEAL, 2019).

American Sign Language

American Sign Language		
Name of Instrument	**Age Range**	**Possible Use**
American Sign Language – Expressive Skills Test (ASL-EST)	4-13 years	The goal of the ASL-EST is to evaluate a child's capacity to create a signed story using proper ASL grammar. To conduct this test, training is necessary. This test is a useful

		instrument for obtaining linked ASL.
American Sign Language – Receptive Skills Test (ASL-RST)	3-13 years	The ASL-RST offers recordings of people utilizing different grammatical structures in ASL. It makes it possible to gauge a child's comprehension of concepts like number/distribution, negation, noun/verb distinction, spatial verbs, size/shape defined, classifiers, role-shifting, and conditionals. It is a grammatical receptive exam, and in order to get a complete picture of the child's language abilities, it should be administered with another test that assesses the child's use of linked ASL.
Assessment, Evaluation, and Programming System for Infants and Children (AEPS)	Birth-6 years	The evaluation instrument employed by Indiana Early Intervention, First Steps is the AEPS. In eight key areas— fine motor, gross motor, adaptive, socialemotional, social-communication, cognitive, literacy, and math—it assesses how well young children are developing.

Center American Sign Language Checklist	K-12th grade	Based on the Indiana Language Standards and the Gallaudet ASL standards, the ASL Checklist is a criterion-referenced language tracking tool created by Center personnel. It gives access to a zone of nearby learning. It is a useful tool for continual tracking but not for thorough analysis. It can support a strong linguistic defense.
Developmental Assessment of Young Children 2nd Edition - Center/ODDACE adaptation (DAYC-2)	Birth-5 years	The DAYC-2 measures five areas of development: cognitive, communication, social-emotional, physical, and abilities for adaptive behavior. Setting objectives using a norm-referenced tool and tracking very young children are both beneficial. It is useful to use with children for the transition from part C to B assessments who may be considerably delayed, shy to work with new people, or difficult to follow adult-led activities. It enables parent interviews and observation.
SKI-HI Language	Birth-5 years	With young children and their families, the LDS is a criterion-referenced language

Development Scale (LDS)		evaluation technique that may be employed. It is a technique used during parent interviews to help determine a child's current level of function in both spoken and signed language.
Test of Narrative Language – Second Edition (TNL-2)	4-15 years	The TNL-2 is a norm-referenced exam that evaluates young learners' narrative language skills, or their capacity to comprehend and narrate tales. A crucial component of language that lays the groundwork for literacy is narration. This is a useful tool for learning about the intricacy and connectedness of a child's language.
Test of Problem Solving 3 Normative Update (TOPS-3:NU)	6-12 years	TOPS-3:NU In elementary school, students are encouraged to use language to reason and think. Language competency is a general measure of how well a kid can think, reason, solve problems, infer, classify, associate, predict, identify causes and sequences, and comprehend instructions. This test is a useful option for observing a

| | | child's connected language and figuring out whether they have academic language abilities or the capacity to think in language. |
| *Visual Communication and Sign Language Checklist (VCSL)* | Birth-5 years | The VCSL is a norm-referenced checklist that offers details on the ASL development of young children. |

Language Assessment: Spoken English

Name of Instrument	Age Range	Possible Use
Assessment, Evaluation, and Programming System for Infants and Children (AEPS)	Birth-6 years	The evaluation instrument employed by Indiana Early Intervention, First Steps is the AEPS. Fine motor, gross motor, adaptive, social-emotional, social-communication, cognitive, literacy, and numeracy development of young children are all assessed.
Assessment of Literacy and Language (ALL)		In addition to language, phonological awareness, alphabetic knowledge, print awareness, fluency (reading), and listening comprehension (story), the ALL examines a child's spoken and written language. It is a useful technique for looking at difficulties with auditory memory. When a DHH youngster struggles with speech's less noticeable sounds, it might be helpful as well.

Comprehensive Assessment of Spoken Language, Second Edition (CASL-2)	3-21 years	There are 14 possible subtests on the CASL-2 that assess spoken English. It has subsections that will examine unintentionally learnt abstract language. It excludes comprehension exercises that could shed light on auditory memory. If a child's language development is many years behind, it could be a wise decision. If the offered answer analysis is used, it can provide qualitative information that aids in goal-writing.
Clinical Evaluation of Language Fundamentals: Preschool 3rd Edition (CELF:P-3)	3-6 years	A number of the CELF:P-3's subtests can reveal information about a DHH student's hearing, expressive grammar, memory, and capacity for differentiating the less noticeable speech sounds. It evaluates early literacy, pragmatics, and language use for thought.
Clinical Evaluation of Language Fundamentals – 5th Edition (CELF-5)	5-21 years	The age ranges for the CELF-5 are 5-8 years and 9-21 years. It has subtests that can reveal information about a DHH child's comprehension of speech sounds and auditory memory.
Clinical Evaluation of Language Fundamentals Metalinguistics – 5th Edition (CELF5-Meta)	9-21 years	Print stimuli are provided by the CELF5-Meta. It examines four areas of language that are frequently picked up by accident. It can shed light on drawing conclusions, metaphorical language, and numerous meanings.

		A score below average on any one subtest reveals linguistic deficiencies that have an influence on the development of higher-level literacy.
Developmental Assessment of Young Children 2nd Edition (DAYC-2)	Birth-5 years	The DAYC-2 measures five areas of development: cognitive, communication, social-emotional, physical, and abilities for adaptive behavior. The use of a norm-referenced measure to follow very young children and set goals is a useful tool. It is useful for children who may be considerably delayed, wary of working with new people, or unable to follow adult-led activities when they move from part C to part B examinations. It enables parent interviews and observation.
Diagnostic Evaluation of Variations (DELV)	4-9 years	The DELV is a diagnostic tool that uses norms to identify speech and language impairments in children who speak English dialects. The four areas covered by the DELV are phonology, pragmatics, semantics, and syntax. It aids educators in reducing evaluation bias against speakers of non-mainstream English dialects. These subtests are helpful in determining when a DHH student is lacking the more subdued dialectal sounds.

Preschool Language Scales 5th Edition (PLS-5)	0-6 years	The PLS-5 is intended to assess the expressive and receptive language skills of young children. This instrument tends to raise scores while having weak psychometric and validity characteristics. If used in conjunction with a thorough language sample, it can be a helpful tool for learning more about a child's language development.
Receptive, Expressive, and Social Communication Assessment – Elementary (RESCA-E)	5-12 years	Information on receptive, expressive, and social language is provided by the RESCA-E. It encompasses social language inference (figurative language), scenario utilization, vocabulary, listening to instructions, understanding tales, describing, and explaining. This program offers a wide range of data regarding a child's linguistic abilities, especially that which is discovered accidentally. Given the duration of the administration, some kids might not be able to use this instrument. Some of it can be translated into ASL.
Test of Early Language Development 3rd Edition/ 4th Edition	2 ½-6 years (3rd) 3-6	The TELD is a brief assessment that might reveal additional surface-level data regarding a child's expressive and receptive

	years (4th)	language skills. It is particularly helpful when used with a young kid who may find it difficult to focus on lengthier testing materials, and it should be used in conjunction with a strong language sample.
Test of Integrated Language & Literacy (TILLS)	6-18 years	The TILLS is a thorough, norm-referenced assessment that has been standardised for three purposes: to recognize language/literacy problems, to record patterns of relative strengths and weaknesses, and to monitor changes in language and literacy abilities over time. It is a good option for getting a broad picture of linked language since it has significant psychometric features. The youngster must be able to use their technology to process recorded aural information because some subtests contain computer audio. It sheds light on narrative abilities, auditory memory, and language use in thought.
Test of Language Development: Primary-	4-8 years	The TOLD:P-5 includes three extra subtests in addition to the six core subtests that assess different facets of spoken

5th Edition (TOLD:P-5)		language. The results of these subtests may be added together to provide composite scores for the three main aspects of language: listening, organizing, and speaking; semantics and grammar; and general language competence. Examiners can use this test to see whether a kid has any possible difficulties with auditory memory, if they are missing any little, less noticeable speech sounds, and if they are capable of using language to think. It has very little visual backing.
Test of Language Development: Intermediate-5th Edition (TOLD:I-5)	8-17 years	The TOLD:I-5 measures several components of spoken language with six core subtests and three supplementary subtests. The results of these subtests may be added together to provide composite scores for the three main aspects of language: listening, organizing, and speaking; semantics and grammar; and general language competence. Examiners can use this test to see whether a kid has any possible difficulties with auditory memory, if they are missing any little, less

		noticeable speech sounds, and if they are capable of using language to think. It has very little visual backing.
Test of Narrative Language 2 (TNL2)	4-15 years	The TNL-2 is a norm-referenced exam that evaluates young learners' narrative language skills, or their capacity to comprehend and narrate tales. The foundation for literacy is laid through narration, a significant part of spoken language that is typically not examined by spoken language examinations. This is a useful tool for learning about the intricacy and connectedness of a child's language.
Test of Problem Solving3: Normative Update (TOPS 3:NU)	6-12 years	Focus is placed on the student's linguistic capacity for thought and reasoning in TOPS 3 Elementary. Language competency is a general measure of how well a kid can think, reason, solve problems, infer, classify, associate, predict, identify causes and sequences, and comprehend instructions. This exam is a good option for seeing a child's connected language and

		figuring out whether they have academic language abilities or the capacity to think in language.

Alternative Supplemental Options for Language Evaluations. Spoken English

These instruments are monitoring and assessment tools for spoken English. Information from teachers and parents may be extremely helpful in assisting DHH youngsters in realizing their full potential. Rating scales, which by their very nature are arbitrary, shouldn't be used in place of a reliable linguistic assessment, but they can offer further information to help with goal setting.

Name of Instrument	Age Range	Possible Use
Children's tion Checklist 2ⁿᵈ C-2)	4-16 years	The CCC-2 is a scale for grading parents or caregivers. It enables the rater to discuss the child's social language, vocabulary, sentence structure, and articulation. It has excellent psychometric characteristics. It has ratings that help distinguish between language disorders and pragmatic disorders.
Language Use Inventory (LUI)	18-47 months	A parent/caregiver rating measure with significant psychometric qualities is the LUI. It enables experts to learn more about a young child's theory of mind and language

		use. It aims to teach about the complexity of language usage and comprehension in children.
SKI-HI Language Development Scale (LDS)	Birth-5 years	With young children and their families, the LDS is a criterion-referenced language evaluation technique that may be employed. It is a technique used during parent interviews to help determine a child's current level of function in both spoken and signed language.
Teacher Assessment of Spoken Language (TASL-II)	No age limit	The TASL-II offers advice on how to concentrate on language development while also assisting instructors in evaluating and assessing syntax.

Language Evaluations for Kids with Special Needs. Spoken English

Name of Instrument	Age Range	Possible Use
Communication Matrix	No age limit	Anyone operating at the early stages of communication (0-24 months) or utilizing modalities of communication other than speech or writing can better understand their communication status, progress, and specific requirements with the use of the Communication Matrix. English, Spanish, Czech, Dutch, Chinese

		(traditional), Russian, Korean, and Vietnamese users can access the matrix online. It evaluates nine categories of communicative behavior at seven levels of communication, from pre-intentional behavior to language: refusing/rejecting, requesting more action, requesting new action, requesting more objects, making choices, requesting a new object, requesting an absent object, showing affection, greeting others, offering/sharing, paying direct attention, answering yes/no questions, asking questions, naming things or people, and making comments.
Developmental Assessment of Young Children 2nd Edition (DAYC-2)	Birth-5 years	The DAYC-2 measures five areas of development: cognitive, communication, social-emotional, physical, and abilities for adaptive behavior. It is a useful tool for tracking very young children and helping them set objectives, as well as for children who may be severely delayed, reticent to interact with strangers, or unable to follow adult-led activities as they move from part C to part B

		examinations. It enables parent interviews and observation.
Early Functional Communication Profile (EFCP)	Birth-10 years	A dynamic assessment instrument called the EFCP is used to compile data on fundamental communication abilities. It is intended to identify particular communication aim, social interaction, and shared attention impairments. The exact descriptive metrics of this criterion-referenced tool reveal what students CAN achieve and how they react to various sorts of challenges..
Oral and Written Language Scales 2nd Edition (OWLSII)	3-21 years	The LC and OE Scales assess receptive and expressive language. The test gives a general overview of language and does not include aspects to assist with determining the ability to access less salient sounds of speech. If the advanced analysis is completed, the OWLSII can provide information on the linguistic structures of semantics, syntax, pragmatics, and supralinguistics.

Test for Auditory Comprehension of Language – 4th Edition (TACL-4) & Test of Expressive Language (TEXL)	3-12 years	To receptively assess semantics, grammatical morphemes, and complex phrases, the TACL-4 offers three visual options. It is a fantastic option for a youngster who requires image help and has major language impairments. It need to be used in conjunction with the expressive language partner measure TEXL, which also assesses semantics, grammatical morphemes, and complex sentences with visual accompaniment.

Benchmark Evaluations

Name of Instrument	Age Range	Possible Use
Dynamic Indicators of Basic Early Literacy Skills (DIBELS)	K-6th grade	The DIBELS are a set of 1-minute developmental assessments that include the following tasks: identifying the alphabetic letters, decomposing words into phonemes, reading fictitious words, reading genuine words, and accurately and fluently reading aloud a book. The sole purpose of DIBELS scores is for instructional decision-making

		(i.e., identifying children who require greater instructional help and tracking intervention response).
Fountas and Pinnell Benchmark Assessment Systems (BAS)	K-8th grade	Teachers use the BAS method to individually assess each student to establish their reading ability.
Indiana's Alternative Measure (I AM)	3rd grade- HS	Indiana's Content Connectors, which are in line with the Indiana Academic Standards, are used by I AM to monitor student development and accomplishment. I AM is the final accountability test for children in grades 3–8 and in high school who have substantial cognitive challenges.
Indiana Learning Evaluation Readiness Network (ILEARN)	3rd – 8th grade	The summative accountability test for Indiana students in grades 3 through 8 and high school biology is called ILEARN. The Indiana Academic Standards for English/language arts (grades 3-8), mathematics (grades 3-8), science (grades 4 and 6) and social studies (grade 5) are used by ILEARN to monitor student accomplishment and progress.

Indiana Reading Evaluation and Determination (IREAD-3)	3rd grade	The grade 3 reading test IREAD-3 was created in compliance with state law. IREAD-3 is developed to evaluate fundamental reading abilities in accordance with Indiana Academic Standards for grades 3 through 8.
Indiana Student Performance Readiness and Observation of Understanding Tool (ISPROUT)	Birth-K	From infancy until kindergarten, skill development in children is assessed using ISPROUT. Social and emotional, knowledge and skill, and independence/motor coordination are the three skill categories that are reported.
i-Ready	K-8th grade	The i-Ready Diagnostic is an adaptive test that modifies its questions based on the requirements of your student. Based on the response to the preceding question, each item a student sees is tailored to them specifically.
Northwest Evaluation Association Measures of Academic Progress Test (NWEA MAP)	K-12th grade	The measurements used by NWEA are known as Measures of Academic Progress (MAP®). The complexity of each question on these computerized adaptive assessments depends on how effectively a student responds

		to all the prior questions. The questions get harder as the student provides right answers. The questions get simpler if the student provides a false response.
STAR Early Literacy	K-3rd	Early literacy and early numeracy are both measured by Star Early Literacy.
STAR Reading	K-12th grade	Star Reading evaluates pupils' reading and vocabulary knowledge, comprehension, and vocabulary application skills.
World-Class Instructional Design and Assessment (WIDA) ACCESS	K-12th grade	WIDA is a tool created for students learning English as a second language to assess their spoken and written language expression in order to inform education.

Scenarios

Examiners should match their techniques with observations, strong language/discourse samples, and narrative examples while monitoring language. Despite having an average overall language score on a norm-referenced assessment, DHH children may still require additional language interventions. Individual subtests that assess language a kid inadvertently learns may result in below-average results, indicating a potential lack of fundamental knowledge necessary for future development of literacy. Even if their results are below average, DHH youngsters still require linguistic coaching.

Frequently Asked Questions (FAQs)

- *How can I monitor my students' language if I offer them the gold standard?*

  usage instruments that will provide information regarding language learnt incidentally, such as measures that look at language memory, usage of grammar, complexity of language, and utilizing language for thinking, in conjunction with norm-referenced assessment and a strong language/discourse and narrative sample. Tests like CELF, TOLD, TILLS, ALL, DELV, RESCA, and others may be helpful for spoken language. ASL-RST, ASL-EST, TOPS-3:NU, and TNL are all beneficial for ASL.

- *My student has a lot of extra needs?*

  Utilize instruments that can monitor gradual improvements, such as the Early Functional Communication Profile or the Communication Matrix. These can be used to spoken English or ASL.

- *My student seems to have excellent language skills, yet she still has reading difficulties.*

  Choose language tools that allow you to use language for thinking and accidental information learning, such as TILLS, TOLD, the Supralinguistic Index of CASL2, CELF5-Meta, TOPS-3:NU, etc. The TOPS3:NU is a useful tool for ASL.

- *My pupil scores poorly on conventional language tests and seems to have highly delayed language abilities.*

  Use a language program like TACL-4/TEXL combo, OWLSII, or CASL2 that has a wider age range and image support. However, they can also indicate the need for extra visual supports and language processing accommodations to assist the kid develop their language. Keep in mind that these tools and supports may result in higher results than what is seen in the classroom.

- ***Parents of my youngster raise worries, but the personnel at the school doesn't detect any linguistic problems?***
  Choose a language-intensive test for the student, such as TILLS, TOLD, RESCA, CELF5-Meta, etc. Give the parents a CCC-2 or LUI checklist that examines social skills and theory of mind as well.

Benefits of Speech, Language Communication Assessment
Having a speech, language, and communication assessment has several advantages, including the following:

- Advice for enhancing communication
- Focused feedback based on assessment findings
- Improved comprehension of requirements thanks to a profile of strengths and challenges
- Developing communication skills to interact with people
- Following intervention, there was an improvement in speech sound production and understandability.

The Rights and Responsibilities of Test Takers: Guidelines and Expectations

According to (American Speech-Language-Hearing Association., 2002) *As a test taker, you have the right to:*

1. Be informed of your rights and responsibilities as a test taker.

2. Be treated with courtesy, respect, and impartiality, regardless of your age, disability, ethnicity, gender,

national origin, religion, sexual orientation or other personal characteristics.

3. Be tested with measures that meet professional standards and that are appropriate, given the manner in which the test results will be used.

4. Receive a brief oral or written explanation prior to testing about the purpose(s) for testing, the kind(s) of tests to be used, if the results will be reported to you or to others, and the planned use(s) of the results. If you have a disability, you have the right to inquire and receive information about testing accommodations. If you have difficulty in comprehending the language of the test, you have a right to know in advance of testing whether any accommodations may be available to you.

5. Know in advance of testing when the test will be administered, if and when test results will be available to you, and if there is a fee for testing services that you are expected to pay.

6. Have your test administered and your test results interpreted by appropriately trained individuals who follow professional codes of ethics.

7. Know if a test is optional and learn of the consequences of taking or not taking the test, fully completing the test, or canceling the scores. You may need to ask questions to learn these consequences.

8. Receive a written or oral explanation of your test results within a reasonable amount of time after testing and in commonly understood terms.

9. Have your test results kept confidential to the extent allowed by law.

10. Present concerns about the testing process or your results and receive information about procedures that will be used to address such concerns.

As a test taker, you have the responsibility to:

1. Read and/or listen to your rights and responsibilities as a test taker.

2. Treat others with courtesy and respect during the testing process.

3. Ask questions prior to testing if you are uncertain about why the test is being given, how it will be given, what you will be asked to do, and what will be done with the results.

4. Read or listen to descriptive information in advance of testing and listen carefully to all test instructions. You should inform an examiner in advance of testing if you wish to receive a testing accommodation or if you have a physical condition or illness that may interfere with your performance on the test. If you have difficulty comprehending the language of the test, it is your responsibility to inform an examiner.

5. Know when and where the test will be given, pay for the test if required, appear on time with any required materials, and be ready to be tested.

6. Follow the test instructions you are given and represent yourself honestly during the testing.

7. Be familiar with and accept the consequences of not taking the test, should you choose not to take the test.

8. Inform appropriate person(s), as specified to you by the organization responsible for testing, if you believe that testing conditions affected your results.

9. Ask about the confidentiality of your test results, if this aspect concerns you.

10. Present concerns about the testing process or results in a timely, respectful way, if you have any.

Rights of Test Takers: Guidelines for Testing Professionals

Test takers have the rights described below. It is the responsibility of the professionals involved in the testing process to ensure that test takers receive these rights.

1. Because test takers have the right to be informed of their rights and responsibilities as test takers, it is normally the responsibility of the individual who administers a test (or the organization that prepared the test) to inform test takers of these rights and responsibilities.

2. Because test takers have the right to be treated with courtesy, respect, and impartiality, regardless of their age, disability, ethnicity, gender, national origin, race, religion, sexual orientation, or other personal characteristics, testing professionals should:

    a. Make test takers aware of any materials that are available to assist them in test preparation. These materials should be clearly described in test registration and/or test familiarization materials.

    b. See that test takers are provided with reasonable access to testing services.

3. Because test takers have the right to be tested with measures that meet professional standards that are appropriate for the test use and the test taker, given the manner in which the results will be used, testing professionals should:

    a. Take steps to utilize measures that meet professional standards and are reliable, relevant, useful given the intended purpose and are fair for test takers from varying societal groups.

    b. Advise test takers that they are entitled to request reasonable accommodations in test administration that are likely to increase the validity of their test scores if they have a disability recognized under the

Americans with Disabilities Act or other relevant legislation.

4. Because test takers have the right to be informed, prior to testing, about the test's purposes, the nature of the test, whether test results will be reported to the test takers, and the planned use of the results (when not in conflict with the testing purposes), testing professionals:

   a. Give or provide test takers with access to a brief description about the test purpose (e.g., diagnosis, placement, selection, etc.) and the kind(s) of tests and formats that will be used (e.g., individual/group, multiple-choice/free response/performance, timed/untimed, etc.), unless such information might be detrimental to the objectives of the test.

   b. Tell test takers, prior to testing, about the planned use(s) of the test results. Upon request, the test taker should be given information about how long such test scores are typically kept on file and remain available.

   c. Provide test takers, if requested, with information about any preventative measures that have been instituted to safeguard the accuracy of test scores. Such information would include any quality control procedures that are employed and some of the steps taken to prevent dishonesty in test performance.

   d. Inform test takers, in advance of the testing, about required materials that must be brought to the test site (e.g., pencil, paper) and about any rules that allow or prohibit use of other materials (e.g., calculators).

   e. Provide test takers, upon request, with general information about the appropriateness of the test for its intended purpose, to the extent that such information does not involve the release of proprietary information. (For example, the test taker might be told, "Scores on this test are useful in predicting how successful people will be in this kind of work" or "Scores on this test, along with other information, help us to determine if students are likely to benefit from this program.")

f. Provide test takers, upon request, with information about re-testing, including if it is possible to re-take the test or another version of it, and if so, how often, how soon, and under what conditions.

g. Provide test takers, upon request, with information about how the test will be scored and in what detail. On multiple-choice tests, this information might include suggestions for test taking and about the use of a correction for guessing. On tests scored using professional judgment (e.g., essay tests or projective techniques), a general description of the scoring procedures might be provided except when such information is proprietary or would tend to influence test performance inappropriately.

h. Inform test takers about the type of feedback and interpretation that is routinely provided, as well as what is available for a fee. Test takers have the right to request and receive information regarding whether or not they can obtain copies of their test answer sheets or their test materials, if they can have their scores verified, and if they may cancel their test results.

i. Provide test takers, prior to testing, either in the written instructions, in other written documents or orally, with answers to questions that test takers may have about basic test administration procedures.

j.   Inform test takers, prior to testing, if questions from test takers will not be permitted during the testing process.

k.   Provide test takers with information about the use of computers, calculators, or other equipment, if any, used in the testing and give them an opportunity to practice using such equipment, unless its unpracticed use is part of the test purpose, or practice would compromise the validity of the results, and to provide a testing accommodation for the use of such equipment, if needed.

l.   Inform test takers that, if they have a disability, they have the right to request and receive accommodations or modifications in accordance with the provisions of the Americans with Disabilities Act and other relevant legislation.

m.   Provide test takers with information that will be of use in making decisions if test takers have options regarding which tests, test forms or test formats to take.

5.   Because that test takers have a right to be informed in advance when the test will be administered, if and when test results will be available, and if there is a fee for testing services that the test takers are expected to pay, test professionals:

a.   Notify test takers of the alteration in a timely manner if a previously announced testing schedule changes, provide a reasonable explanation for the change, and inform test takers of the new schedule. If there is a change, reasonable alternatives to the original schedule should be provided.

b.   Inform test takers prior to testing about any anticipated fee for the testing process, as well as the fees associated with each component of the process, if the components can be separated.

6. Because test takers have the right to have their tests administered and interpreted by appropriately trained individuals, testing professionals should:

   a. Know how to select the appropriate test for the intended purposes.

   b. When testing persons with documented disabilities and other special characteristics that require special testing conditions and/or interpretation of results, have the skills and knowledge for such testing and interpretation.

   c. Provide reasonable information regarding their qualifications, upon request.

   d. Insure that test conditions, especially if unusual, do not unduly interfere with test performance. Test conditions will normally be similar to those used to standardize the test.

   e. Provide candidates with a reasonable amount of time to complete the test, unless a test has a time limit.

   f. Take reasonable actions to safeguard against fraudulent actions (e.g., cheating) that could place honest test takers at a disadvantage.

7. Because test takers have the right to be informed about why they are being asked to take particular tests, if a test is optional, and what the consequences are should they choose not to complete the test, testing professionals should:

   a. Normally only engage in testing activities with test takers after the test takers have provided their informed consent to take a test, except when testing without consent has been mandated by law or governmental regulation, or when consent is implied by an action the test takers have already taken (e.g., such as when applying for employment and a personnel examination is mandated).

b. Explain to test takers why they should consider taking voluntary tests.

c. Explain, if a test taker refuses to take or complete a voluntary test, either orally or in writing, what the negative consequences may be to them for their decision to do so.

d. Promptly inform the test taker if a testing professional decides that there is a need to deviate from the testing services to which the test taker initially agreed (e.g., should the testing professional believe it would be wise to administer an additional test or an alternative test), and provide an explanation for the change.

8. Because test takers have a right to receive a written or oral explanation of their test results within a reasonable amount of time after testing and in commonly understood terms, testing professionals should:

a. Interpret test results in light of one or more additional considerations (e.g., disability, language proficiency), if those considerations are relevant to the purposes of the test and performance on the test, and are in accordance with current laws.

b. Provide, upon request, information to test takers about the sources used in interpreting their test results, including technical manuals, technical reports, norms, and a description of the comparison group, or additional information about the test taker(s).

c. Provide, upon request, recommendations to test takers about how they could improve their performance on the test, should they choose or be required to take the test again.

d. Provide, upon request, information to test takers about their options for obtaining a second interpretation of their results. Test takers may select an appropriately trained professional to provide this second opinion.

e. Provide test takers with the criteria used to determine a passing score, when individual test scores are reported and related to a pass-fail standard.

f. Inform test takers, upon request, how much their scores might change, should they elect to take the test again. Such information would include variation in test performance due to measurement error (e.g., the appropriate standard errors of measurement) and changes in performance over time with or without intervention (e.g., additional training or treatment).

g. Communicate test results to test takers in an appropriate and sensitive manner, without use of negative labels or comments likely to inflame or stigmatize the test taker.

h. Provide corrected test scores to test takers as rapidly as possible, should an error occur in the processing or reporting of scores. The length of time is often dictated by individuals responsible for processing or reporting the scores, rather than the individuals responsible for testing, should the two parties indeed differ.

i. Correct any errors as rapidly as possible if there are errors in the process of developing scores.

9. Because test takers have the right to have the results of tests kept confidential to the extent allowed by law, testing professionals should:

    a. Insure that records of test results (in paper or electronic form) are safeguarded and maintained so that only individuals who have a legitimate right to access them will be able to do so.

    b. Should provide test takers, upon request, with information regarding who has a legitimate right to access their test results (when individually identified) and in what form. Testing professionals should respond appropriately to questions regarding the reasons why such individuals may have access to test results and how they may use the results.

    c. Advise test takers that they are entitled to limit access to their results (when individually identified) to those persons or institutions, and for those purposes, revealed to them prior to testing. Exceptions may occur when test takers, or their guardians, consent to release the test results to others or when testing professionals are authorized by law to release test results.

    d. Keep confidential any requests for testing accommodations and the documentation supporting the request.

10. Because test takers have the right to present concerns about the testing process and to receive information about procedures that will be used to address such concerns, testing professionals should:

    a. Inform test takers how they can question the results of the testing if they do not believe that the test was administered properly or scored correctly, or other such concerns.

b.   Inform test takers of the procedures for appealing decisions that they believe are based in whole or in part on erroneous test results.

c.   Inform test takers, if their test results are under investigation and may be canceled, invalidated, or not released for normal use. In such an event, that investigation should be performed in a timely manner. The investigation should use all available information that addresses the reason(s) for the investigation, and the test taker should also be informed of the information that he/she may need to provide to assist with the investigation.

d.   Inform the test taker, if that test taker's test results are canceled or not released for normal use, why that action was taken. The test taker is entitled to request and receive information on the types of evidence and procedures that have been used to make that determination.

The Responsibilities of Test Takers: Guidelines for Testing Professionals

Testing professionals should take steps to ensure that test takers know that they have specific responsibilities in addition to their rights described above.

1.   Testing professionals need to inform test takers that they should listen to and/or read their rights and responsibilities as a test taker and ask questions about issues they do not understand.

2.   Testing professionals should take steps, as appropriate, to ensure that test takers know that they:

   a.   Are responsible for their behavior throughout the entire testing process.

b. Should not interfere with the rights of others involved in the testing process.

c. Should not compromise the integrity of the test and its interpretation in any manner.

3. Testing professionals should remind test takers that it is their responsibility to ask questions prior to testing if they are uncertain about why the test is being given, how it will be given, what they will be asked to do, and what will be done with the results. Testing professionals should:

a. Advise test takers that it is their responsibility to review materials supplied by test publishers and others as part of the testing process and to ask questions about areas that they feel they should understand better prior to the start of testing.

b. Inform test takers that it is their responsibility to request more information if they are not satisfied with what they know about how their test results will be used and what will be done with them.

4. Testing professionals should inform test takers that it is their responsibility to read descriptive material they receive in advance of a test and to listen carefully to test instructions. Testing professionals should inform test takers that it is their responsibility to inform an examiner in advance of testing if they wish to receive a testing accommodation or if they have a physical condition or illness that may interfere with their performance. Testing professionals should inform test takers that it is their responsibility to inform an examiner if they have difficulty comprehending the language in which the test is given. Testing professionals should:

a. Inform test takers that, if they need special testing arrangements, it is their responsibility to request appropriate accommodations and to provide any requested documentation as far in advance of the testing date as possible. Testing professionals should inform test takers about the documentation needed to receive a requested testing accommodation.

b. Inform test takers that, if they request but do not receive a testing accommodation, they could request information about why their request was denied.

5. Testing professionals should inform test takers when and where the test will be given, and whether payment for the testing is required. Having been so informed, it is the responsibility of the test taker to appear on time with any required materials, pay for testing services and be ready to be tested. Testing professionals should:

a. Inform test takers that they are responsible for familiarizing themselves with the appropriate materials needed for testing and for requesting information about these materials, if needed.

b. Inform the test taker, if the testing situation requires that test takers bring materials (e.g., personal identification, pencils, calculators, etc.) to the testing site, of this responsibility to do so.

6. Testing professionals should advise test takers, prior to testing, that it is their responsibility to:

a. Listen to and/or read the directions given to them.

b. Follow instructions given by testing professionals.

c. Complete the test as directed.

d. Perform to the best of their ability if they want their score to be a reflection of their best effort.

e. Behave honestly (e.g., not cheating or assisting others who cheat).

7. Testing professionals should inform test takers about the consequences of not taking a test, should they choose not to take the test. Once so informed, it is the responsibility of the test taker to accept such consequences, and the testing professional should so inform the test takers. If test takers have questions regarding these consequences, it is their responsibility to ask questions of the testing professional, and the testing professional should so inform the test takers.

8. Testing professionals should inform test takers that it is their responsibility to notify appropriate persons, as specified by the testing organization, if they do not understand their results, or if they believe that testing conditions affected the results. Testing professionals should:

   a. Provide information to test takers, upon request, about appropriate procedures for questioning or canceling their test scores or results, if relevant to the purposes of testing.

   b. Provide to test takers, upon request, the procedures for reviewing, re-testing, or canceling their scores or test results, if they believe that testing conditions affected their results and if relevant to the purposes of testing.

   c. Provide documentation to the test taker about known testing conditions that might have affected the results of the testing, if relevant to the purposes of testing.

9. Testing professionals should advise test takers that it is their responsibility to ask questions about the confidentiality of their test results, if this aspect concerns them.

10. Testing professionals should advise test takers that it is their responsibility to present concerns about the testing process in a timely, respectful manner.

Summary

Age-appropriate reading, spelling, and/or writing difficulties are indicative of language-based learning disorders. This may involve problems with reading comprehension and writing expression.

Receptive language disorders make it difficult for children to comprehend spoken and written language. A youngster who struggles with expressive language has a hard time communicating with others and expressing their emotions. There are several potential reasons of language difficulties, including brain damage and birth defects.

References

Al-Balas HI, Abuhalaweh M, Melhem HB, Al-Balas H. . (June 2021;). Conversion disorder with aphonia in 12 years old male patient: A case report. . *Int J Surg Case Rep.* , 84:106135. doi:10.1016/j.ijscr.2021.106135.

American Psychiatric Association. . (2013). *Diagnostic and statistical manual of mental disorders: Fifth Edition.* . Arlington,: VA: American Psychiatric Association. .

American Speech-Language-Hearing Association. (2002). *Rights and responsibilities of test takers: guidelines and expectations [Relevant Paper].* Available from www.asha.org/policy.

Bariroh, S. (2018). The Influence of Parents' Involvement on Children with Special Needs' Motivation and Learning Achievement. *International Education Studies*, Vol. 11, No. 4; 2018.

Bussmann, H. (1996). *Routledge dictionary of language and linguistics* . London: (pp. 37, 71, 92, 311, 335). , UK:.

Coleman, C. (2013). *SIGnatures: widening the treatment circle. Involving parents enhances treatment for children who stutter. So why not include the child's siblings, friends, teachers and other communication partners?* . The ASHA Leader, 18, 54-56.

Elkind, D. (1986). *Formal Education and Early Childhood Education: An Essential Difference.* . Phi Delta Kappan, 67.

Fuandai, C. M. (2010). Catering For Children With Special Needs In The Regular Classroom: Challenges And The Way Forward. *Edo Journal of Counselling*, Vol. 3, No. 1,.

IDEA. (2004). *Part C: Evaluation and Assessment Definitions.* https://www.asha.org/advocacy/idea/idea-part-c-evaluation-and-assessment-definitions/.

IDEAL. (2019). *Center for Deaf and Hard of Hearing Education. Reporting results can be logged within the* . portal at https://eportal.isdh.in.gov/CDHHEAssessmentPortal/.

Oluremi, D. (2015). Counselling Intervention and Support Programmes for Families. *Journal of Education and Practice*, Vol.6, No.10, 2015.

Pachaiappan C, Sangeetha G, Balasubramanian S, Ramya Sri C. (May 2020;). Treating functional aphonia: A case study. *Int. J. Health Res.* , 2249-9571., 10(5). ISSN:.

Robinson, H. &. (1968). *The problem of timing pre-school education" in Hess, R.D and bear, R.M (Eds) Early education,* . Illiois:: Aldine publishing.

Santrock, J. (2006). *Educational Psychology and Classroom:* . Update New York.: MC Graw Hill.

Saul Mcleod. (2023). *Maslow's Hierarchy Of Needs (1954).* https://simplypsychology.org/maslow.html.

DISORDERS OF LEARNING

Introduction

Learning disorders are brought on by genetic and/or neurobiological factors that change how the brain functions and hence impact one or more learning-related cognitive processes. These processing issues may make it difficult to master fundamental abilities like reading, writing, and/or math. Additionally, they may impair higher order abilities including organization, time management, abstract thought, long or short term memory, and concentration. It's vital to understand that learning difficulties can have an influence on a person's life outside of school, including their connections with family, friends, and coworkers.

Practical, medical, and legal definitions of learning disorders are all possible. The three definitions have one thing in common: a learning impairment is a dysfunction in one or more psychological processes that may show up as a poor aptitude in some learning domains, including reading, writing, or math.

Practical Definition

The term "learning disabilities", sometimes referred to as specific learning disabilities, is an umbrella term that covers a range of neurologically based disorders in learning and various degrees of severity of such disorders. Predecessor terms include: minimal brain damage and minimal brain dysfunction.

Broadly speaking, these disorders involve difficulty in one or more, but not uniformly in all, basic psychological processes:

- Input (auditory and visual perception),
- Integration (sequencing, abstraction, and organization),

- Memory (working, short term, and long term memory),
- Output (expressive language), and
- Motor (fine and gross motor).

Learning disabilities vary from individual to individual and may present in a variety of ways. Learning disabilities may manifest as difficulty:

- Processing information by visual and auditory, means, which may impact upon reading, spelling, writing, and understanding or using language,
- Prioritizing, organizing, doing mathematics, and following instructions,
- Storing or retrieving information from short or long term memory,
- Using spoken language, and
- Clumsiness or difficulty with handwriting.

Learning disabilities are not emotional disturbances, intellectual disabilities, or sensory impairments. They are not caused by inadequate parenting or lack of educational opportunity.

Cognitive assessment, including psycho-educational or neuropsychological evaluation, is of critical importance in diagnosing a learning disability.

Learning disabilities may be diagnosed by qualified school or educational psychologists, by clinical psychologists, and by clinical neuropsychologists who are trained and experienced in the assessment of learning disabilities.

Medical Definition

A category for Specific Learning Disorder may be found in the section on Neurodevelopmental Disorders in the draft Fifth Edition of the Diagnostic and Statistical Manual of Mental Disorders (DSM-V). Motor and Communication Disorders are included in the section on neurodevelopmental disorders. The draft DSM-V's

Specific Learning Disorder includes issues with reading comprehension, written language, and mathematical reasoning.

Reading disorder, mathematics disorder, disorder of written expression, and learning disorder not otherwise specified (NOS) are all included in the current DSM-IV-TR.

Legal Definition

The definition of "specific learning disability" according to the Individuals with Disabilities Education Act (IDEA) is "a disorder in 1 or more of the basic psychological processes involved in understanding or in using language, spoken or written, which disorder may manifest itself in the imperfect ability to listen, think, speak, read, write, spell, or do mathematical calculations." As stated in the definition, this phrase "includes such conditions as perceptual disabilities, brain injury, minimal brain dysfunction, dyslexia, and developmental aphasia." This phrase excludes "a learning problem that is primarily the result of intellectual disabilities, emotional disturbance, visual, hearing, or motor disabilities, or of environmental, cultural, or economic disadvantage." 30. 20 U.S.C. Section 1401.

The Americans with Disabilities Act (ADA) does not explicitly define "learning disabilities," but courts have cited the IDEA language in ADA-related cases.

An issue arises when a youngster struggles in school. When children struggle with schoolwork, parents and teachers may get concerned about the obstacles inhibiting learning. It's true that underachievement in school is one of the most typical causes for a visiting specialist to be referred to a school or to a counseling center for kids. However, underachievement may be a sign of various cognitive, emotional, and social challenges.

Reading difficulties have been identified as the primary factor in school failure. Reading problems are really a common factor in the failure of many students in other subjects. Various categories have been used to group kids with reading difficulties. (Mansour, 2003) Used the term strephosymbolia to refer a learning problem in which symbols and especially phrases, words, or letters appear to be reversed or swapped in reading. Later, terms like minor brain dysfunction, alexia, and word blindness were adopted. The word dyslexia has recently been used to describe kids with reading learning problems. This name was first offered to describe kids who struggle with reading because of neurological issues. However, it is presently being employed in many different contexts, such as the identification of genetic causes for reading difficulties.

Since Morgan (1896) made the first reference of reading difficulties in children in the literature, a variety of methods, resources, strategies, and possible causes have been looked into and studied. Experts from a wide variety of disciplines, including medicine and education, have contributed their knowledge in an effort to better understand these children.

The focus of the medical community has been etiology. As a result, doctors typically assume that a child's dyslexic behavioral patterns are being caused by some sort of brain abnormality. However, many educators hold the view that there are a number of additional explanations for reading difficulties, not the least of which is ineffective or unsuitable training. However, the main focus of many educators is to simply pinpoint the inadequate reading habits and afterwards impart the proper reading techniques (Pennington BF, 2006).

Specific Learning Difficulties

An individual with a specific learning challenge (SLD) has a difference or difficulty with one or more particular aspects of learning. Children and teenagers with SLDs are still capable of learning and succeeding in school.

The discrepancy criteria, which classify a kid as having an SLD if their achievement is below what would be anticipated based on general cognitive ability, have been the most widely used method for diagnosing specific learning challenges (SLDs) for a long time. In fact, the discrepancy model is adopted by the two primary categorization systems used in clinical practice at the time of writing, ICD-10 (World Health Organization) and DSMIV (American Psychiatric Association). However, the discrepancy approach's application in educational settings has steadily decreased because there is no proof that children with SLDs who have higher or lower IQs have different etiologies or prognoses (Snowling, 2008)

As a result, the DSM-5 plan, which we shall examine below, departs from this strategy. The response to intervention approach, an alternative categorization method that is gaining popularity and has advantages for low- and middle-income countries, will also be taken into consideration.

The methods used by the diagnostic systems to identify SLDs vary. DSM-IV is less clear than ICD-10 on the length of time that must pass before a diagnosis is accepted, and in DSM-5, it is suggested that the discrepancy formula be completely abandoned.

The way co-morbidities are handled in different diagnostic systems also varies. Co-occurring issues are diagnosed in parallel in DSMIV and DSM-5. The diagnostic is attached to one nodal issue or cluster of difficulties in the ICD-10 hierarchy of co-occurring difficulties. The classification of a co-occurring challenge might sometimes have an impact on how well we understand its etiology (for example, literacy and language difficulties that co-occur or follow one another).

The labels for the many learning-related issues that are frequently used in educational settings don't always match the clinical diagnoses because all of these diagnostic systems are based on medical models. Examples of clinical diagnoses that don't neatly suit what is seen in typical classrooms are provided below:

<table>
<tr>
<td></td>
<td>

Specific Spelling Issues.
In some writing systems (where reading is regular but spelling-sound mappings are uneven), spelling issues are more prevalent than reading difficulties. Poor spelling typically co-occurs with reading difficulties.

</td>
</tr>
<tr>
<td>

Disorder of Written Expression
This condition is not adequately diagnosed. This is due less to the fact that it might be challenging to recognize weak writing abilities and more to the perception that writing problems are secondary to reading and spelling issues.

</td>
<td>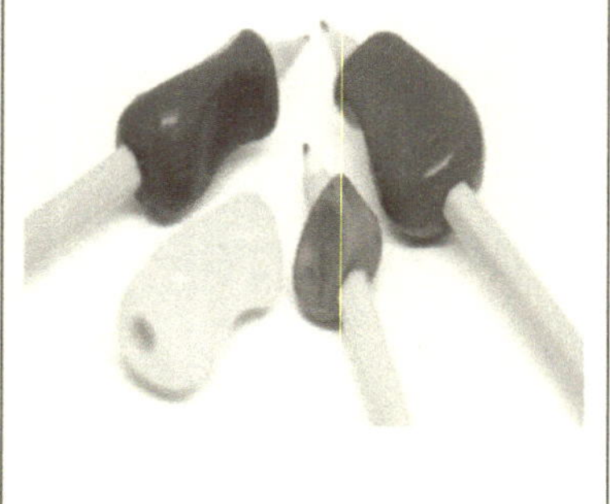</td>
</tr>
</table>

Furthermore, certain diagnostic labels are general words and are therefore useless for intervention. For instance, reading comprehension problems and reading accuracy problems are included together in the DSM-IV and ICD-10, respectively.

However, these issues call for different treatments: whereas reading comprehension treatments emphasize expanding spoken language and inferential abilities, treatments for reading accuracy generally rely on phonological abilities.

Approaches to Specific Learning Disabilities

ICD-10	DSM-IV	Proposed for DSM-V
• Disorders include combined disorders of academic skills (81.3), disorders of arithmetic skills (81.2), Disorders of reading (81.0), and disorders of spelling (81.1).	• Developmental reading disorder (315.00), math disorder (315.1), and disorder of written expression (315.2) are among the disorders.	• The general term for conditions marked by challenges with academic skill acquisition is learning disorder. accurate and fluid writing, reading, and math skills, which considerably impair everyday functioning or academic performance
• The lowered attainment must not be attributable to a lack of opportunities for qualified literacy instruction or other external factors like disrupted schooling and recent entry into regular school.	• The child's level of learning must be significantly lower than that of peers who have had comparable opportunities.	• Communication difficulties and learning disabilities are clubbed together. Diseases to represent the commencement of their neurodevelopmental counterparts throughout the years of pre- or early-school
• Instead, it must be due	• When a known sensory deficit, such as nystagmus or low vision, coexists with the underachievement, the extent of the learning delay should be significantly greater than the known contribution of the sensory deficit. • The lower levels of achievement must be seen to be	• Dyslexia and dyscalculia are two examples of the learning disorders listed in DSM-5. &

to differences in the child's performance on individually administered tests that are two or more standard errors below predictions based on age and general intelligence.

- This criteria indicates irregularity in fundamental cognitive abilities and a potential biological rather than sociocultural or environmental cause for the issue.

interfering with academic achievement and daily living. All co-morbidities, including attention impairments, emotional issues, and behavioral disorders, should be reported. The co-occurring difficulty must also be classified.

- Reduced self-esteem and self-efficacy for academic achievement, as well as higher hurdles for admission into school, postsecondary education, and the workforce, are known to occur together with other related social-emotional issues.

- The DSM-IV recommends the documentation of these and

a lack of organization in writing

- The proposed deletion of the inconsistency criteria in DSM-5. Reading fluency will be acknowledged for the first time as a diagnostic evaluation factor (previous manuals only mentioned reading accuracy).

- This modification matches the current knowledge of the clinical picture of dyslexia; in many languages, poor reading fluency (rather than reading accuracy) is a distinguishing characteristic of dyslexia. In most languages, low reading fluency is known to be a chronic condition throughout adulthood.

comparable related problems.	• There won't be a clear explanation for particular reading comprehension issues (formerly categorized as reading disorders). It is therefore difficult to diagnose two groups of kids: - Those who have excellent decoding abilities but bad reading comprehension, and - Those who have weak oral language at first but then develop weak reading comprehension. It is observed that the poor comprehender profile is a sign of language impairment and may be categorized under a new heading termed learning disability.

Types of Reading Problems

Whether the reading difficulties are primarily experiential (such as those encountered by English language learners) or related to impairments (such as those common to children with dyslexia), patterns of reading difficulty offer an educationally helpful method to think about the many types of reading challenges.

- **Visual Discrimination**:
  Reading fluency and visual discrimination are strongly related. Fluency is impacted by visual discrimination since one cannot read effectively if they are unable to recognize minute visual differences and similarities. This might prompt someone to read the words or text again if they were hard for them to distinguish visually.

  Although most of us are aware that visual discrimination is a fundamental reading ability, we rarely consider the link between fluency and discrimination.

  The capacity to recognize minute differences and similarities visually is known as visual discrimination. This is how we are able to see the specifics of what we are observing. What is similar? What's altered? Details to consider are colors, sizes, and shapes. As you go over these characteristics in depth, you will be able to interpret the meaning of the phrase by defining the words and letters.

  "Form constancy" is an extra component of visual discrimination. The capacity to identify things when they are seen from a different perspective is known as form constancy. For instance, regardless matter whether I am looking at a shoe from the top, the side, or the bottom, it is still a shoe. Books are form-consistent as well. A book is a book no matter how you look at it. Not every letter has form consistency, though.

Form constancy is the capacity to maintain spatial location while simultaneously recognizing visual similarities and contrasts. Not all letters exhibit form stability, although the majority do. For instance, the shapes of a "b," "d," "p," and "q" are all the same. Now that the form has been reversed, it is a different letter. With the letters "W" and "M," the same thing takes place. Frequently mistaken are the letters S and the number 5. Furthermore, a letter's location in relation to another letter affects its appearance. The discriminating procedure also takes into account the arrangement of letters within words.

A lot of kids who struggle with reading aren't able to distinguish between different letters or words. Letters having similar configurations, such h-n, I-j, and v-w, may confound a youngster struggling in this area. Other kids who struggle with visual discrimination aren't able to tell words apart visually.

The following are indicators of visual discrimination:

- Mismatch between the characters and the digits
- Finding information on open-book quizzes difficult reading aloud and losing their spot
- Difficulty appreciating puzzles and reading;
- Difficulty identifying subtleties and distinctions

- **Auditory discrimination:**
Auditory discrimination gradually develops in preschool age and the ability to determine sounds in words correctly is a prerequisite to learning to read. At the beginning of first grade, children can syllabify words, determine the first and last letter in words (very soon they will learn to spell whole words), perceive vowel length and discriminate between similar-

sounding but different words. All of this belongs to the category of so-called phonemic awareness (phoneme = speech sound).
One of the major characteristics of children with auditory disturbances in reading is the inability to differentiate between phonemic sounds. The ability to distinguish similarities and differences among words is also closely associated with this skill.

This ability is often weakened in individuals with dyslexia and causes reading difficulties for almost all of them, or writing difficulties in individuals with dysorth98'
ography (these two kinds of difficulties usually go hand in hand, only in certain age one might get slightly more prominent than the other – in Czech it is definitely more difficult to learn to write correctly than to speak).

Although these people's hearing is impeccable, when they are to precisely determine similar-sounding sounds and tones, it's like they don't "hear" the difference, or even when they get older, they must stop to think about it to be able to determine it; they don't realize the difference automatically.

And the same thing happens with the awareness of sounds in words – they perceive and understand the word as a whole perfectly, but the precise determination of every single sound is difficult for them. However, we need phonemic awareness not only when writing a word, but also when we see a written word composed of speech sounds, because it is thanks to phonemic awareness that we can figure out how to pronounce it. That's why children in primary school diagnosed with dyslexia learn to spell words and work with speech sounds (to determine vowel length, distinguish between soft and hard syllables, etc.).

Sometimes this skill develops very well with training, but it is still not fully automated for fast reading and writing, and that's why some mistakes may still appear. An important precaution that might make working easier is to provide enough time for both of these activities, so that the individual could take time to think how to read a certain word (especially in case of foreign and less common words) or how to write it. Very often, these problems manifest to a greater extent when learning foreign languages or encountering unknown words (e.g. technical terms we have never heard before).

- **Sound Blending:**
This is the ability to synthesize sound into a complete word. Children with this difficulty are unable for example to blend 1+1 into word math. The three phonemes or this word remain as separate sound. According to (Ellis Richardson, Barbara DiBenedetto and C. Michael Bradley, 1977) a child will encounter reading problems if sounds cannot be synthesize into words, even if the child knows all the sounds.

- **Memory Skills:**
Children with memory disturbances experience difficulty in recalling information that has been learned. Young children can develop the habit of becoming active readers to improve working memory while they read. When reading long novels, encourage your kid to highlight, underline, or make notes on important points in the margin. Students may also gather and jot down their thoughts regarding the book using sticky notes on sheets. Reading the material aloud to your child is a fantastic way to help them comprehend and remember what they have read. Together, you can take "mental notes" throughout the reading aloud by debating the meaning of certain words or passages, pausing to emphasize important concepts and terms, or both. memory skills in reading include the ability to:

  - Retain impressions or traces of visual and auditory stimuli.

- Make comparisons with past auditory and visual experiences.
- Store and retrieve grapheme phoneme correspondences.

New terms and concepts are much easier to recall when they are categorized. According to several studies, children are twice as likely to remember related words when category cues are used as opposed to when they are left to remember them on their own.

After reading a book, try your hand at some category games. Assist your youngster in remembering new concepts and words. Ask your kid to list all the animals they can think of, including any new ones they may have learnt from the book, if the book has any animal illustrations. You may consider classifying them according to several factors, such where they reside or how many legs they have.

Ask your youngster to summarize the main points of a book you've read to you soon after. They can create a synopsis, illustrate the events, or just tell you what happened chronologically. Inquiries can also be used to reaffirm important details in the text. Asking questions such as "Where did the dog find his family?" "Why do you think the boy felt sad about moving houses?" or "What would have happened if the day had been rainy instead of sunny?" might help spark a post-reading conversation.

- **Letter and Word Reversals:**
  A widely discussed characteristics of children with reading disabilities is the tendency of many children to read (or write) some letters and words backwards, rotated, or inverted single letters such as b, d, p, q, n, u, m, and w are often among the letter symbols which are read upside down and backwards.

- **Word Analysis Skills:**
One of the most important skills for learning to read adequately is the ability to analyze words effectively. Adequate word analysis skills are usually judged by the versatility of techniques utilized by the reader. Among the many word analysis techniques available, phonics is probably the most widely used technique. However, structural analysis, configuration, picture clues, sight vocabulary and contextual analysis should also be used by the efficient reader.

- **Sight Words:**
Words which a reader can recognize instantly are referred to as sight words. Some words appears over and over again in basic reading material e.g: said, you, all. The ability to recognize these words immediately facilitates early achievement in reading.

The child who is unable to recognize some words at sight will be severely limited in reading. (Paul Mupa, Tendeukai Isaac Chinooneka, 2015) Also suggests that he or she may develop many unfortunate reading habits, perhaps including word guessing, very slow reading, substituting words, and constantly losing the place.

In addition, the child with an inadequate sight vocabulary will probably rely upon phonic analysis of words for many non-phonetic words.

- **Literal Comprehension Skills:**
Many of the comprehension skill deficits that are observed among the reading disabled may be classified as literal comprehension difficulties. (Quigley, 2020) refer literal comprehension as recall of directly state facts. Some of the

skills involved in literal reading include noting specific facts and details, understanding words and paragraphs, recalling sequence of events. Following direction, skimming reading to locate specific information, and grasping the main idea.

Children with literal comprehension difficulties might find it difficult to locate or recall specific reading passages which describe a person, place, or thing reading for details or recalling particular facts to answer specific question might also be frustrating.

- **Interpretive Comprehension Skill.**
  In contrast to literal skills, interpretive comprehension involves those skills which go beyond the printed page, including critical judgments.

  The ability to make inferences, predict outcomes and from opinions are other kinds of interpretive comprehension skills. The majority of interpretive abilities must be considered higher cognitive mental processes.

  Many learning disabled children have comprehension disturbances because of cognitive difficulties. The difficulties that are experienced in these areas are frustrating to the child and teacher alike.

- **Critical Reading Skill:**
  Reading critically is a more ACTIVE kind of reading. It is a more in-depth and intricate reading experience.
  Analyzing, interpreting, and occasionally assessing texts is the process of critical reading. When we read critically, we QUESTION the material and how we read it by applying our critical thinking abilities. Certain fields of study may have their own unique approaches to critical reading (scientific, philosophical, literary, etc.).

Critical reading is a type of comprehension which involves critical and value judgment based on the attitudes and experiences of the reader.

It is usually considered the highest level of comprehension when the reader analyzes and evaluated the reading material. Some skills included under critical reading are Judging accuracy, drawing conclusions, distinguishing between fact and opinion, and evaluating the authority intentions and beliefs. (Heick, 2022) Suggest that Reading closely and carefully in order to completely comprehend and evaluate a text is known as critical reading. Critical reading necessitates reading slowly and carefully, considering the audience, purpose, and structure of the text in addition to other elements (such as tone, mood, diction, etc.). It is not only about skimming or reading for story points.

Reading books with the goal of completely understanding them is known as critical reading. It entails raising concerns regarding the meaning of certain words and phrases, the structure and goal of the work, and the author's intention. Critical readers also take into account how a piece could be understood by various audiences and the context in which it was created. The reader must engage the material in a dialogue at the critical reading level in which he compares the printed material with other material. Or with the total conceptual background he possesses.

Conclusion

When the brain processes information in a non-typical fashion, it is called a learning disorder. It prevents someone from picking up and mastering a skill. The majority of people who suffer from learning difficulties are intelligent, if not exceptionally so. Thus, there is a discrepancy between their academic performance and the predicted skills based on their age and IQ.

Understanding speech is the foundation of reading. Reading learning difficulties are sometimes caused by a child's inability to comprehend spoken words as a combination of unique sounds. Understanding how a letter or letters convey a sound and how letters form words may become challenging as a result.

References

Elkind, D. (1986). *Formal Education and Early Childhood Education: An Essential Difference.* . Phi Delta Kappan, 67.

Ellis Richardson, Barbara DiBenedetto and C. Michael Bradley. (1977). The Relationship of Sound Blending to Reading Achievement. *American Educational Research Association*, Vol. 47, No. 2 (Spring, 1977), pp. 319-334 (16 pages) .

Hyman, S.L., Levy, S.E., Myers, S.M., & AAP . (2020). *Council on Children with Disabilities, Section on developmental and behavioral pediatrics. Identification, evaluation, and management of children with autism spectrum disorder.* . Pediatrics, 145(1), e20193.

IDEA. (2004). *Part C: Evaluation and Assessment Definitions.* https://www.asha.org/advocacy/idea/idea-part-c-evaluation-and-assessment-definitions/.

IDEAL. (2019). *Center for Deaf and Hard of Hearing Education. Reporting results can be logged within the* . portal at https://eportal.isdh.in.gov/CDHHEAssessmentPortal/.

Karine Tremblay, D. L. (2012). *Assessment Of Higher Education Learning Outcomes. Feasibility Study Report Volume 1.* https://www.oecd.org/education/skills-beyond-school/AHELOFSReportVolume1.pdf.

Kirk, S. A., Gallagher, J. J., Anastasiow, N. J., & Coleman, M. R. (2006). *Educating Exceptional Children (11th ed.).* Boston,: MA: Houghton Mifflin.

Kostelink, M.J., Whiren. A.P., Soderman, A.K. & Gregory, K. . (2006). *Guiding children's social development: Theory to practice.* . U.S.A.: : Thomson Delmar learning.

Quigley, A. (2020). *Closing the reading gap.* . Routledge.

Snowling, M. (2008). Specific disorders and broader phenotypes:The case of dyslexia. ,. *Quarterly Journal of Experimental Psychology*, 61:142-156.

Stipek, D.; Feiler, R.; Daniels, D.; Milburn, S.;. (2013). *Effects of different instructional approaches on young children's achievement and motivation.* ISSN : 0009-3920 vol. 66.

Tarnopol, L. a. (1977). *Brain Function and Reading Disabilities.* . Baltimore: : University Park Press.

Treiman, R. (2018). *What research tells us about reading instruction. Psychological Science in the Public Interest,.* 19(1), 1–4. https://doi.org/10.1177/1529100618772272.

Winebenner, S. (2008). *D. Demers adaptation of Teaching Kids with Learning Difficulties in the Regular Classroom entitled Enseigner aux élèves en difficulté en classe régulière.* . Montreal: Les Éditions de la Chenelière.

www.ingramcontent.com/pod-product-compliance
Lightning Source LLC
LaVergne TN
LVHW040013200726
843493LV00005B/1249